FLYING SCOREBOARDS

Aircraft Mission and Kill Markings

By Ernest R. McDowell

Color by Don Greer &
Tom Tullis

 **squadron/signal publications**

A P-51 Mustang of the 111th Tactical Reconnaissance Squadron (Snoopers), 68th Tactical Reconnaissance Group in Algeria during the Fall of 1943 used an "eyeball" marking on the side of the fuselage to indicate each photo reconnaissance mission flown. The Yellow bands on the wing were recognition markings to help identify the Mustang to friendly crews.

ISBN 0-89747-305-1 First Edition

If you have any photographs of aircraft, armor, soldiers or ships of any nation, particularly wartime snapshots, why not share them with us and help make Squadron/Signal's books all the more interesting and complete in the future. Any photograph sent to us will be copied and the original returned. The donor will be fully credited for any photos used. Please send them to:

Squadron/Signal Publications, Inc.
1115 Crowley Drive.
Carrollton, TX 75011-5010

Photo Credits

C.M. Barnes	S. Birdsall
P. Bowers	COL J.W. Boyce
Mark Bacon	J. M. Campbell
LCOL C. Cook	M. Cross
J.V. Crow	F. D'Amico
L. Davis	F. C. Dickey
M.J. Eppstein	J. Ethell
J.O. Field	G. L. Frey
R. Fry	J. P. Gallagher
C. Graham	J. L. Grimm
J. C. Hanna	T. Heinonen
W. N. Hess	R.M. Hill
S. Hilosky	L. J. Hickey
R. C. Jones	C. Joy
D. A. Kasulka	K. Kistler
G. C. Kohn	A. Krieger
P. J. Litteau	A. Makiel
R. C. McWherter	D. W. Menard
P. Moewe	CAPT B. Moore II
D. Musikoff	N. A. Nilsson
K. Niska	E. Obie
D. Packham	B. Philipott
P. J. Quilty	N. Rajala
P. D. Stevens	H. H. Stapfer
B. Shadbolt	S. Smith - Haskell
R. J. Soutar	V. C. Tannehill
M. Toda	H. Valtonen
R. Winkle	B. Widfeldt
D. Weatherill	P. Yant
N. J. Waters III	USAF Museum
USAF	LCOL W. Watson
USAAF	USN
Boeing	Kesiki-Suomen Ilmailmuseo
T.M. Lore	

Dedication

To my family: Mary, Paul, Donna, Donald and Betsy and to Stubby, Chuckles, Tinker, Boom Boom, Corky and Duffy — the little pooches who have brightened our lives.

MAJ Gleen T. Eagleston of the 354th Fighter-Bomber Group was the top scoring ace in the 9th Air Force with eighteen and a half kills. His P-47D Thunderbolt carried his scoreboard as simple German crosses with the half kill marked as half a cross. He later added two kills to his credit in Korea. (USAF)

INTRODUCTION

...At some point back in the prehistoric period a man must have decided to boast of his prowess as a hunter or warrior by selecting some tangible method to publicly show how skillful or fierce he proclaimed himself to be. What form this took will never be known but it could have been the tooth of a saber-toothed tiger, the skin of some animal or perhaps the head of an enemy of his tribe.

History does recount the use of scalps, shrunken heads and other such items for this purpose. As man became more civilized he had to forsake such grisly means and rather than display the remains of his victory, he decided to use personal ornamentation. Fierce head dress and masks, warpaint, tattoos and other similar items served to show others how great a warrior he was.

As warfare advanced the need for larger groups to be recognized as either friend or foe brought about the development of uniforms and in time these became very colorful and distinctive. Mention the Bengal Lancers, the U.S. 7th Cavalry, the Black Watch, Cossacks, Coldstream Guards, U.S. Marine Corps, French Foreign Legion, or the Green Berets and a picture of a man in a particular uniform quickly comes to mind and conveys the idea that he was part of an elite organization with a sense of pride and a strong esprit de corps.

It was this type of background and the need for recognition that was responsible for the use of victory and mission markings on aircraft that began during the First World War and have been carried forward to this day.

WORLD WAR I

Once aerial combat was introduced into the conflict it was only a matter of time until some young aviator would find some method of showing just how successful in combat he had become. The first military award for an aerial combat victory was devised and awarded by Germany. The Germans created the Ehrenbecher (Honor Cup) which

This Spad XIII of the 22nd Aero Squadron carries a circle around the shooting star squadron emblem that consists of ten German iron cross emblems one for each of CAPT Jacques M. Swaab's ten air-to-air victories.

This SPAD XIII of the 22nd Aero Squadron carries forty-four White tombstones each marked with a Black Germany cross. This system was used to identify the entire squadrons score. (Via Fred C. Dickey)

was awarded, along with a citation signed by a high ranking officer, to the pilot, observer, or machine gunner upon confirmation of his first aerial victory. The award was made only once in an aviators career. The Ehrenbecher was made to hold one liter of wine with which to toast the victors skill. The base of the cup was inscribed "Der Selger in Luftkampf" (The victor in air combat) and a pair of eagles were etched on the cup, one with wings extended was hovering over the other which was depicted in a fallen position. Initially the cups were silver but later, due to wartime shortages, iron was substituted for silver. Among the pilots who received the Ehrenbecher was Manfred von Richtofen and it may have been the inspiration for his personal collection of victory symbols. He decided to award himself a small silver cup for each victory and on those sorties when he achieved a double kill he instructed his jeweler to make the cup double the size.

While there are not many examples of personal victory markings and perhaps none to indicate number of sorties flown during the war, a few examples were recorded by photographers of the period. The 93rd Aero Squadron kept a running record of their success by tacking a strip of dope lined fabric across the door of their operations room. "One Victory Roll" was painted next to the squadron's Sioux Indian head emblem across the top. Beneath it columns were set up in which the pilot's name and date of his victory were recorded. The 1st Day Bombardment Group used a smiliar scoreboard that was headed "Enemy Planes Confirmed." They ran the columns horizontally across the scoreboard with each

CAPT Victor H. Strahm flew this Salmson 2A2 of the 91st Aero Squadron. Strahm, a native of Evanston, Illinois and his observer were credited with the destruction of five enemy aircraft, for which he was awarded the DSC. Their score was carried on the knights shield in the form of four German crosses at the top of the shield and another cross at the bottom. (Via Fred C. Dickey)

This Salmson 2A2 of the 91st Aero Squadron, aircaraft number 5, was credited with the destruction of three Greman aircraft. The crew used Black German iron cross markings on the shield of the squadron insignia to indicate their victories. Like Rickenbacker they also marked bullet holes in their aircraft with a White patch that had a Black cross painted on it. These are visible, one under the knight and the other between the struts just behind the pilot. (Via Fred C. Dickey)

squadron's emblem on the left side and a stylized German cross for each victory. They ran the crosses eight to a line and added a second line when necessary. The squadrons were listed in ascending order by number: 11th, 20th, 96th, and 166th.

CAPT Eddie Rickenbacker had his mechanic paint a White circle over the patch where an enemy bullet had penetrated his Spad and add a German cross to the center. A Salmson squadron also used the same marking on their planes to indicate where they had been holed by enemy shells.

The 22nd Aero Squadron had at least three different Spads that carried rows of small White tombstones marked with a Black cross in a straight row along the bottom of the fuselage. The total of these victory symbols stood at forty-six. Photographic coverage show that aircraft numbered 0, 20, and 25 carried these markings and it is possible that others or even the entire squadron may have had them.

Salmson crews seem to have been the first to carry individual victory markings. CAPT D. H. Arthur and his observer 1LT H.E. Feason of the 12th Aero Squadron, flying a Salmson 2A2 named OLD CAROLINA IV carried three German crosses on the bomb clutched in the talons of the hawk of the squadron emblem to denote their three kills. CAPT Victor H. Strahm of the 91st Aero Squadron was a Salmson Ace, a rare feat for an observation crew. The squadron emblem was a knight on horseback with a shied and lance chasing a devil. CAPT Strahm used the shield as a scoreboard putting four crosses across the top and a lone cross at the bottom. This may have been done to show the pilot's and observer's victories seperately. Another 2A2 of the 91st (aircraft number 5) carried three crosses in a diagonal line on the shield. This Salmson also had White rectangular patches over bullet holes and, like Rickenbacker's Spad, they had a Black cross painted in the center of the patch.

Victory markings were applied to Rickenbacker's Spad after the Armistice just prior to shipping it back to the United States. These were applied to his Spad XIII sometime before 6 March 1919 as it was photographed on that date showing twenty-six crosses during a visit to Lay St. Remy. Due to the large number of crosses, only seven were painted on the hatband inside the hat, the rest were shown spilling out of it.

CAPT Reed M. Chambers, Commander of the 94th Aero Squdron, was an ace with seven victories, stands beside his "American Flag" Spad XIII (this wild color scheme was not applied until after the end of the war). The inside hat band featured seven Black crosses to indicate his score and a number of other pilots also painted their Spads with their kills recorded in the hat band with the appropriate number of Black crosses.

CAPT Edward V. Rickenbacker of the 94th Aero Squadron alongside his SPAD XII. Rickenbacker had his mechanic leave the small round patches that he used to cover machine gun bullet holes unpainted and later had them painted with a small Black iron cross so they would show up better. At the end of the war this SPAD was to be shipped back to the states for display. While at Lay St. Remy on 6 March 1919 he visited the 138th Aero Squadron and the Hat in the Ring insignia had twenty-six iron crosses added, seven on the inner band and the rest spilling out of the hat in rows of four, four, five, four and two to complete the twenty-six kill scoreboard. (Via Fred C. Dickey)

Officially CAPT Eddie had only been credited with twenty-five victories at that time. Victory crosses inside the hatband also appeared on a number of other 94th Aero Squadron Spads that had been painted in really gaudy markings and paint schemes for an air show as a part of the First World War victory celebration. They included the Spads of CAPT Reed M. Chambers, LT Leo Dawson, LT Harvey Weir, LT Robert Donaldson, LT Dudley "Red" Outcault, LT Sammy Kaye, LT Willie Palmer, LT John E. Jeffers and LT Pat Maloney.

The credit for being first to use victory markings of a personal nature has to be given to pilots of observation aircraft rather than pursuit pilots.

LT William W. Palmer was another of the 94th Aero Squadron pilots who elected to use a diamond motif to dress up his Spad XIII. His aircraft was overall White with Red and Blue diamonds. He had three Black crosses in the hat band indicating his confirmed score of three kills.

LT Arthur Raymond Brooks of the 22nd Aero Squadron named his Spad XIII (No. 7689) SMITH IV. The aircraft was displayed during 1919 at Romorantin, France with the total victory tally of the squadron carried along the bottom of the fuselage in the form of a White tombstone with a Black cross for each enemy aircraft destroyed. SMITH IV was named after CAPT Brooks girlfriends college since he did not relish the idea of having to write home that Ruth had her tail shot up. So he passed up naming his Spad after her.

5

LT Robert W. Donaldson had his SPAD XIII painted overall White with Black checkers with the exception of the undersurfaces of the wings and tailplane. Donaldson's hat insignia featured a lone German iron cross in the inner hat band. The hat was trimmed in Black and the band was a solid color. (Via Fred C. Dickey)

(Left) LT Weir Cooks had his Spad XIII painted overall Black with Orange lightning flashes. Cook had seven victories and these were painted on the inside sweat band of the Uncle Sam hat insignia of the 94th Aero Squadron. The lighting flashes were different on the left and right fuselage sides and were also used on the wings. The Ring was outlined in White so it would stand out against the Black fuselage. (Via Fred C. Dickey)

This SPAD XIII of the 138th Aero Squadron at Coblenz, Germany after the war was painted in Red, White and Blue diamonds. The 138th painted their fuselage insignia over the aircraft's original markings (the 94th Aero Squadron). (via Fred C. Dickey)

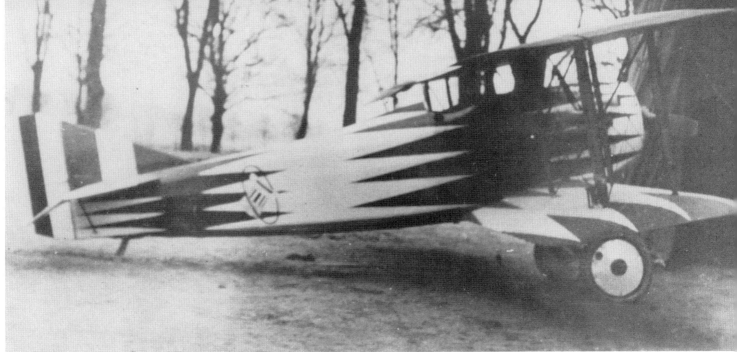

This Spad XIII of the 94th Aero Squadron carried a colorful scheme as part of the post war victory celebrations. The Hat in the Ring insignia is carried further back on the fuselage side. (Via Fred C. Dicky)

LT John N. Jeffers of the 94th Aero Squadron had his SPAD XIII painted in an unusual scheme that resembled the Japanese flag. The center of the flag held a five pointed star on a Blue circle with a Red center (similar to U.S. post war markings). The disc had a thin Red surround. The entire aircraft was painted a pale Blue and the radiating stripes alternated between Red and White. The Hat sweat band carried two iron crosses for his two victories. (Via Fred C. Dickey)

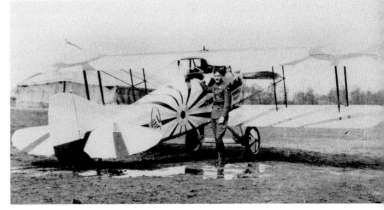

LT Leo H. Dawson in the cockpit of "Little Joe" which was painted in Green stripes and shamrocks. The name "Little Joe" appeared just above the exhaust stack in White on a Green rectangle along with a pair of dice with the two deuces up under the name. The 94th insignia had a Green background on this ship. He had a White shamrock on the Green wheel cover. He carried four Black iron crosses on the inside hat band to indicate his score. (Via Fred C. Dickey)

Reed Chamber's SPAD XIII was turned over to the 138th Aero Squadron and flown by MAJ Maxwell Kirby at Fort Alexander, Coblenz, Germay. The squadron took part, along with the 41st, 141st and 638th Squadrons of the 5th Pursuit Group in the Third Army Carnival held between 23- 27 April 1919. Stunt flying, acrobatics, and message dropping contests were held and on the last day a German balloon was used as a target and shot down. (Via Fred C. Dickey)

WORLD WAR II

As might be expected, in the beginning of America's involvement in the Second World War markings, when they came into widespread usage, were relatively simple with bomb symbols for missions and Japanese flags for enemy aircraft destroyed. As U.S. forces were depolyed to Europe the practice was carried on there with Swastikas and Fascist symbols replacing the Rising Sun symbols for German and Italian aircraft destroyed.

During the early days in the European Theater of Operations (ETO) missions were so rough that some crews viewed the bomb mission symbols in the same light as that of a prisoner who was checking off the days left on his sentence on a calendar in his cell. Their magic number was twenty-five in the beginning and that was a number many crews unfortunately were never to see on their aircraft.

As the war wore on the odds became more favorable and the men's outlook became less grim. Traditional American individuality asserted itself and new symbols came into use that were limited only by the imagination of crews. In many cases these reflected the type of mission flown, the enemy involved and even the names they painted on their aircraft.

In due time the senior officers in positions of command came to realize that these symbols were good for the morale of both air and ground crews, tended to build pride and were also good for building civilian morale when used in news reels and home town newspapers. Most of the nations involved in the Second World War used such symbols in pretty much the same manner with variations according to their cultures.

The British took a rather dim view of victory markings feeling that their usage on the aircraft of top scoring aces would draw extra attention from the enemy. There were a few examples but these kept the victory markings to a minimum size. The Russians forbade the use of the swastika as a kill marking so fierce was their hatred of the enemy symbol. They did, however, allow a Free French squadron to use the iron cross as victory symbols but these were limited in size. Russian aces normally used Red stars to record their victorys. Japanese fighter pilots used a variety of marking styles, as did the Finns. Germans mainly used a slender bar, often with the national insignia of the enemy superimposed on it. Since their aces scored so many kills they simply painted the number and their highest decoration award on the fin or rudder of their aircraft. The Italians used markings on both fighters and bombers.

This P-38 Lightning of the 20th Fighter Grop carried twenty-two mission markings on the nose. The markings consisted of White bombs covered with umbrellas, indicating the missions were top cover for bombers. (J. Campbell)

Since few if any regulations were laid down many variations existed in every nation, many of which probably never will be brought to light because photographs were never taken or no longer exist

U.S. Army Air Force
Fighters

Fighter pilots showed that they had a flare for variety in their victory marking. While the fighter-bomber groups had more leeway to add mission symbols,but as the war wore on and other fighter groups began flying more ground attack missions, they began using them as well. Some became pretty much standardized; umbrellas for top cover, brooms for fighter sweeps, top hat and cane for escort, locomotives for train busting bombs for low level fighter-bomber sorties and cameras for reconnaissance missions. Placement of these markings was fairly individual and was another way to get an added bit of variety and be different from your squadron mates. Some used the aircraft nose, others chose the fuselage or around the canopy frame. In the case of the P-39, the door seemed an ideal location. On the P-38, most pilots used the center fuselage pod. In many cases, pilots have told us that their crew chiefs were both happy and proud to be able to add a kill marking and that many of the pilots wished that they could have done better for the sake of their ground crews more than for personal glory.

MAJ Ernest K. Oscher was the commander of the 95th Fighter Squadron and flew SAD SACK, a P-38G-15 Lightning with eight kills and four bombing missions painted on the nose. The SACK finished the war with 183 combat missions, sixteen kills and over 820 combat hours. The Lightning was flown by thirty pilots during its career. (Jeff Ethell)

1LT Richard Loehert and SGT Dickerson point out the full scoreboard on California Cutie, a P-38J-10 Lightning of the 20th Fighter Group. She was credited with six locomotives, fifty-six top hat and cane (escort) missions, nine umbrella (top cover) missions, and eleven broom (fighter sweep) missions. The markings were in White against the aircraft's Olive Drab camouflage. (Royal Frey)

PUTT PUTT MARU was flown by COL Charles H. MacDonald, commander of the 475th Fighter Group. He carried twenty-four Japanese flags painted against a Black background on his P-38J, this practice was also used by other pilots in the 5th Air Force to make their kills stand out. (Via David Weatherill)

JEANNE, a P-38J Lightning of the 55th Fighter Squadron, 20th Fighter Group carried a Black scoreboard with White markings consisting of two locomotives, 1 ship, two aircraft kills, two bombing missions, nine fighter sweeps, two top cover missions and thirty-six escort sorties. (Royal Frey)

STAR EYES was an F-4 Photo Lightning of the 28th Photo Reconnaissance Squadron, 7th Air Force. She carried sixty-five Black camera silhouettes on the nose one for each of her photo reconnaissance missions. (Fred C. Dicky Jr.)

LCOL John H. Lowell of the 384th FS, 364th Fighter Group shows off his fourth kill marking on his P-38J. By the end of the war he added another three and a half kills to his score. The pilots of the 384th did not get too elaborate in their personal markings. J.O. Field)

MAJ McManus and his ground crew in front of *Marie*, a P-38 of the 364th Fighter Group, 67th Fighter Wing at Honnington, England on 15 June 1944. His scoreboard carried forty bomber escort missions and two kill markings. Officially, MAJ McManus was never given credit for the two kills. (USAF)

(Left) *REBEL II* was a P-38J flown by MAJ Moody of the 393rd Fighter Squadron, 367th Fighter Group. The scoreboard showed a total of nineteen bombing missions, nine top cover missions, twenty escort missions and four fighter sweeps. (D. Packham via David Weatherill)

Pearl III carried five White swastika victory markings along with two question marks on the fuselage. The question marks were for the two probable kills credited to this P-38 pilot. (John M. Campbell)

Connie & Butch Inc. was a P-38J-10-LO of the 383rd Fighter Squadron, 364th Fighter Group flown by CAPT George F. Ceullers. At this time he carried three kills on the nose of his Lightning, but by the end of the war he had added another seven and a half kills. (USAF)

This P-38F-15-L Lightning of the 94th Fighter Squadron, 1st Fighter Group has a rather full scoreboard. It was credited with three victories, forty-five bombing missions, and eighty-nine fighter sweeps. The 1st FG was based in the Mediterranean Theater of Operations (MTO). (USAF via Jeff Ethell)

The pilot of this Lockheed F-5 of the 90th Photo Reconnaissance Squadron has a total of thirty-seven Black camera silhouettes on the nose of his Photo Lightning. The camera silhouette was a popular marking for reconnaissance aircraft and saw wide spread use. The 90th was based in North Africa at the time. (USAF via Jeff Ethell)

LCOL Gerald R. Johnson, commander of the 49th Fighter Group flew this P-38 named *Jerry*. He carried an unusual marking in with the twenty-four Japanese flag kill markings, an Australian flag indicating the RAAF reconnaissance aircraft shot down in error due to a communications foul-up, luckily the RAAF pilot survived the incident. (Jim Gallagher)

11

Dear John was a P-38H lightning flown by CAPT Edward R. Newbury of the 27th Fighter Squadron, 1st Fighter Group in North Africa. His scoreboard carries forty-three bombing missions, forty-nine fighter missions (Lightning silhouettes), four enemy aircraft destroyed and one small boat.(Ilfrey via J. Campbell)

LT Royal D. Fry of the 20th Fighter Group carried this scoreboard on his P-38 Lightning indicating two victories, two fighter sweeps, nine bomber escort and eleven top cover missions. (Author)

Gentle Annie was a P-38J flown by COL Harold Rau of the 20th Fighter Group.The aircraft carries five kill markings on the nose under the name, although COL Rau was only credited with a single kill. The White band around the nose was to fool the Germans into thinking this was an unarmed Droop Snoot P-38. The aircraft also carried two small Black bomb symbols.

MAJ R.C. Rogers of the 392nd Fighter Squadron, 367th Fighter Group along side *"LITTLE BUCKEROO"*. The aircraft has thirty-two bombing mission markings and five kill markings. According to official USAAF records, MAJ Rogers did not receive credit for his five kills and is not on the official list of aces. (C. Joy via David Weatherill)

Super Snooper, an F-5 Lightning of the 30th Photo Reconnaissance Squadron, 7th Photo Reconnaissance Group was based at Eschwege, Germany during April of 1945. Her scoreboard had (top to bottom) three high altitude recon missions, four escort missions, nine photo missions and nine dicing missions. (Larry Davis)

"Philbert 3" was a P-38J-25-LO Lightning of the 394th Fighter Squadron, 376th Fighter Group flown by MAJ Charles F. Matheson. His scoreboard consisted of thirty-six bombs, thirteen top hats (escorts), nineteen brooms (fighter sweeps) and a pair of kills. (C. Joy via David Weatherill)

This P-47D Thunderbolt was flown by CAPT Samuel V. Blair of the 341st Fighter squadron, 348th Fighter Group. At this time his Jug had a scoreboard of six Japanese flags (he later added another) CAPT Blair was with Neel Kearby on the mission that cost Kearby his life. One of Blair's Thunderbolts was later recovered from a swamp in New Guinea long after the war.

This P-47D Thunderbolt is armed with three shot rocket tubes under the wings. Its unusual scoreboard consists of thirty (three rows of ten) White sweatsocks. (Robert C. Jones)

CAPT Edward F Reddy of the 342nd Fighter Squadron, 348th Fighter Group carried eight Japanese flag kill markings on the fuselage of his P-47D Thunderbolt. The first row of five are badly weathered while the second row is fresh. His fifth kill was on 17 December and his sixth and seventh came on 26 December, less than ten days later. (USAF)

The damage to the wingtip of this P-47D Thunderbolt of the 9th Air Force was typical of the hazards of the ground attack mission. The aircraft carries forty mission markings consisting of four bombs for dive bombing missions and thirty-six rockets for close support and interdiction missions.

1LT E.G. Obie of the 36th Fighter Group, 9th Air Force and his ground crew show off their scoreboard. The Republic P-47D Thunderbolt has flown over forty-three fighter-bomber sorties (bombs), four fighter sweeps (brooms) and twenty-three top cover missions (high hats). The markings are in Black on the Natural Metal aircraft. (E. G. Obie)

CAPT David Parrish in the cockpit of his P-47D Thunderbolt of the 396th Fighter Squadron, 361st Fighter Group. CAPT Parrish was credited with three victories, however, all that is carried on his Thunderbolt at this time were three bombs superimposed on a broom which were used to indicate fighter-bomber sweep, a common mission late in the war.

"The Vangoose" was a P-47D Thunderbolt of the 356th Fighter Group, 8th Air Force. It carries twenty-three bomb symbols of a slightly different style. The Black bombs were carried on a White scoreboard so that they stood out.

LT Walter A. Grabowski of the 511th Fighter Squadron, 405th Fighter Group, 9th Air Force flew this P-47D Thunderbolt while stationed in Germany during 1945. His scoreboard held 167 fighter-bomber sorties, twenty-four fighter sweeps, thirteen top cover missions and twelve other missions (P-47 silhouettes). (J.V. Crow)

COL Francis S. Gabreski flew with the 56th and 4th Fighter Groups in the European Theater of Operations during the Second World War and with the 51st Fighter Group in Korea. He scored a total of thirty-four and a half kills (6.5 in Korea). COL Gabreski painted the type of each kill over the German flag marking of his camouflaged P-47D Thunderbolt. Eight were Focke Wulf 190s, eight were Messerschmitt Bf-110s, eleven were Messerschmitt Bf-109s and there was a single Messerschmitt Me-210 included in the total of twenty-eight victories. The colors of the German flags were Red, White and Black. (Paul J. Litteau)

LT Morris Williams of the 376th Fighter Squadron, 361st Fighter Group flew this Thunderbolt named DEVIL MAY CARE. His scoreboard included silhouettes of .50 caliber machine gun shells to indicate strafing runs. The shells were Yellow with Red tips.

Anne II was a P-47D Thunderbolt of the 509th Fighter Squadron, 405th Fighter Group, 9th Air Force at St. Dizier, France during 1944. The scoreboard carried eighteen fighter escort missions, thirty fighter-bomber missions, five fighter sweeps and sixteen rockets for close support/ground attack missions. (James V. Crow)

"CORNY BABE" was a P-47D of the 391st Fighter Squadron, 366th Fighter Squadron, 9th Air Force carried eight different types of mission and victory markings, including three tanks, three trains, six top hats for escort missions, five brooms for fighter sweeps, four Buzz bombs and forty bombs. It also carried a single large iron cross for its single air-to-air kill. (James V. Crow)

Daddy RABBIT was a P-47D Thunderbolt with a scoreboard consisting of two kills, fifty bombs, four tanks, five trains, eight brooms (fighter sweeps), fifteen top hats (top cover missions), twenty P-47 silhouettes and nine rabbits. The meaning of the rabbits is unknown and any one's guess. (Larry Davis)

1LT Louis E. Curdes flew BAD ANGEL, a P-51D Mustang (44-63272) of the 4th Air Commando Squadron, 3rd Air Commando Group. LT Curdes' scoreboard includes seven German kills and one Italian kill scored while with the 95th Fighter Squadron in the Medaterrean Theater, and one Japanese kill scored after joining the 3rd Air Commando Squadron. The single American flag was for a C-47 he shot down. The C-47 was about to land by mistake on a Japanese held island and LT Curdes shot out its engines forcing it to ditch. (James P. Gallagher)

LT Jesse B Gray had only two victories on his P-51B Mustang, of the 75th Fighter Squadron, 23rd Fighter Group in China. For some unknown reason he had the two victory symbols painted in a diffent style.

MAJ William A. Shomo of the 82nd Tactical Reconnaissance Squadron had a total of eight victories. seven on a single mission (11 January 1945). Shomo's first kill was scored while flying a Bell P-39 Airacobra. The scoreboard of his F-6D Mustang was a Blue rectangle with Red/White Japanese flags. MAJ Shomo was awarded the Medal of Honor for his action of 11 January. The name *The Flying Undertaker* was in reference to Shomo's civilian occupation. (Ralph Winkle)

CAPT Robert J Goebel of the 308th Fighter Squadron, 31st Fighter Group was one of the high scoring aces of the 15th Air Force. He used the Balkenkruz for his kill markings on his P-51D Mustang. At this time he had eleven kills painted in a row on the fuselage below the cockpit. (David Weatherill)

2LT Clarence D. Lester of the 100th Fighter Squadron, 332nd Fighter Group had three kills on his P-51B Mustang, all scored on the same day 18 July 1944. His scoreboard consisted of simple swastikas on a Red background. (David Weatherill)

2LT Ralph "Kid" Hofer of the 334th Fighter Squadron, 4th Fighter Group also used the Balkenkruz as his victory marking. He scored a total of sixteen and a half kills before he was killed in action on 2 July 1944. (G.L. Fry)

(Right) 1LT Frank Q. O'Conner of the 354th Fighter Group carried a scoreboard on his camouflaged P-51B Mustang that consisted of ten Black swastikas on White backgrounds. His final total was ten and a half victories.

MAJ Robert C. McWherter of the 363rd Fighter Group carried three Japanese flags and three German flags for his six kills. He was officially only credited with four kills, as two of his Pacific kills, claimed while with the 17th Pursuit Squadron on Java, were disallowed after the war. (R.C. McWherter)

LCOL Sidney S. Woods is another ace who carried both Japanese and German kills. He gained his Japanese kills while with the 49th Fighter Group and his German kills were scored while with the 4th Group. His photo was being taken because he had just scored five kills on a single mission. (Via Garry Fry)

(Left) MAJ Leonard K. "Kit" Carson of the 362nd Fighter Squadron, 357th Fighter Group was officially credited with eighteen and a half victories, although only eighteen are shown on the scoreboard of his P-51D Mustang.

Passion WAGON was flown by LT Arval J. Roberson of the 362nd Fighter Squadron. His split scoreboard contained six kills. His score was actually five kills plus two shared kills. His aircraft was a non-standard color of Forest Green instead of the usual Olive Drab. (Via David Weatherill)

CAPT Richard E. Turner flew *SHORT-FUSE SALLEE* of the 354th Fighter Group, 8th Air Force. He carried a total nineteen victory flags on his P-51D. After the war, his total was reduced to eleven confirmed enemy aircraft plus one V-1 kill.

CAPT Charles E. Yeager flew *GLAMOROUS GLEN III* of the 363rd Fighter Squadron. CAPT Yeager carried twelve kill markings on his P-51D Mustang. His final total was eleven and a half victories. (COL Don Bochkay via Phil Yant)

U'VE HAD IT! was flown by MAJ John B. England. This P-51B Mustang (one of four he flew) carried nine victory markings plus twenty-six bomb symbols. He finished the war with a total of eighteen and one half kills. (M. Olmsted)

(Right and Above right) *Peitie 2nd* was the P-51D assigned to LCOL John C. Meyer of the 487th Fighter Group. At one point it carried only eighteen kills on the fuselage under the cockpit. Later a total of twenty-four swastikas were carried on the Mustang. He also gained two MiG kills in Korea.

COL John Landers carried six Japanese flags under the cockpit of his P-51 Mustang gained while with the 49th Fighter Group in the Pacific. In addition he had eleven German kills gained with the 4th Fighter Group in England.

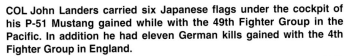

19

CAPT Clarence E. Anderson flew *OLD CROW* with a total of eighteen kills on the scoreboard under the windshield. On his P-51D he used the flag style kill marking, while on his earlier P-51B he used the iron cross style kill marking. (COL D. Bochkay via Phil Yant)

(Left) *RIDGE RUNNER III* was the Mustang flown by MAJ Pierce W. McKennon during May of 1945. He carried twenty kills plus two parachute markings that were used to indicate the two incidents where he was forced to bail out of *RIDGE RUNNER I* and *II*. (Garry L. Fry)

Red DOG XII was a P-51D flown by MAJ Louis H. Norley of the 334th Fighter Squadron. He elected to use swastikas as his victory marking and carried them on the canopy frame. He scored a total of sixteen which included five ground kills. (Norley via G.L. Fry)

"Mrs. Bonnie" was a P-51D flown by LCOL William D. "Bill" Dunham of the 406th Fighter Squadron, 38th Fighter Group on le Shima during August of 1945. His Mustang carried sixteen Japanese flags, a pair of White ship kills and thirty White bomb markings. (J.V. Crow)

(Right) MAJ Jack Ilfrey of the 20th Fighter Group and his ground crew in front of *HAPPY JACK'S GO BUGGY*. His Mustang carried fifty-eight White top hats (escort missions), four brooms (sweeps), five bombs, and four locomotives in addition to his six kills. He later added one more kill to his total. (Larry Davis)

At one time, MAJ Leonard K."Kit" Carson's *Nooky Booky IV* carried twenty-three Black swastikas inside Red circles on the fuselage below the cockpit. Carson was assigned to the 362nd Fighter Squadron, 357th Fighter Group, 8th Air Force. MAJ Carson's official score was eighteen and a half kills.

CAPT Charles E. Weaver of the 362nd Fighter Squadron flew this P-51D Mustang with a scoreboard that consisted of eleven kills (including three ground kills) His kill markings were the Luftwaffe eagle insignia. One of his kills was a Me-262.

THIS IS IT! was flown by Joe L. Mason (second from right) commander of the 352nd Fighter Group. His P-51D carried five iron cross markings for his five kills. (Larry Davis)

MAJ Donald H. Bochkay of the 363rd Fighter Group, 357th Fighter Squadron points to his third victory swastika, which was applied in an unusual shape on his P-51B Mustang. Eventually his scoreboard would consist of some fourteen kills. He also had nine White bomb mission markings on the fuselage below his kills. (J. V. Crow)

CAPT Donald M. Beerbower of the 353rd Figther Squadron, 354th Fighter Group was the 9th Air Force's leading ace before being killed in action on 9 August 1944. His P-51B had a Malcom canopy and carried a total of seventeen kill markings in an usual arrangement. In addition to his air-to-air kills he also carried a White locomotive to denote his destruction of an enemy train. (USAF via Jeff Ethell)

This Mustang carried a unique mission marking. For escort missions the pilot had the silhouette of a B-17 Flying Fortress flanked by a pair of P-51 Mustangs on a rectangle. There were at least four of this type of marking along with several rectangles that had not been filled in. (Art Krieger)

1LT Paul A. Smith was the pilot of *"Lady GEN"* a P-61B of the 422nd Night Fighter Squadron. His radar operator was 1LT Robert E. Teirney and they shared the credit for the six kills painted on the fuselage below the cockpit. In addition they also destroyed six locomotives and a V-1 flying bomb. Their forty-four lightning flash mission markings were carried just behind the radar antenna on the fuselage side. (John A. Campbell)

U. S. Army Air Force
Bombers

Bombers are probably the most interesting subjects for mission markings for several reasons. One, being large they offered plenty of room for large scoreboards. Second, they flew many different types of missions. And third they also scored kills.

While many fighter pilots did not bother to use any type of mission marking, being content simply to show their victories, others, especially those who flew fighter-bomber missions and low level tactical support (and had less chances at downing enemy aircraft) still wanted to have something to show for their work so they were more inclined to use mission symbols, similar to the markings that were common on the bombers.

The bomb symbol became pretty universal to show missions completed and enemy flag markings for kills was also pretty standard. Later, some units or individuals elected to use a silhouette of the enemy aircraft they had downed. Silhouettes of ships, tanks, submarines etc. were also used to denote the destruction of these targets.

The urge to be different seems to exist in all airmen and one of the ways to display it was in these markings. Different colors were used on bomb symbols to denote different types or locations of targets, the Swastika underwent many versions as a kill markings and the locations of these markings was widely varied, limited only by the desires of the crews.

RABID RABBIT was a B-17G of the 483rd Bomb Group that was later transferred to the 99th Bomb Group complete with its crew. The missions markings were added after the aircraft went to the 99th although the nose markings were added while the aircraft was with the 483rd. The mission markings were made up of sixty small rabbits and there was a single swastika for an air-to-air kill. The aircraft also carried a small Red star marking for a shuttle raid to the Soviet Union from Italy. (Steve Hilovsky, 483rd Bomb Group)

DREAM STREET ROSE of the 376th Bomb Group in North Africa carried thirty-six stars to indicate the mission count and the name OLE KING SOLOMON above the stars. The aircraft number 96 identifies ROSE as a member of the 515th Bomb Squadron.

Thundermug, a B-17F-50-B0 (42-29604) Flying Fortress, flew most of its missions with other 5th Bomb Wing Groups, but finished the war with the 483rd Bomb Group. *Thundermug's* scoreboard shows that she flew over 100 missions, claimed nine enemy aircraft destroyed and, although rare for the ETO, sank a ship. (Parke Moewe)

BIG YANK of the 483rd Bomb Group carried fifty Black bomb mission markings on the nose along with the silhouettes of three Me-262 jet fighters above the scoreboard. The crew was credited with destroying two and a half Me-262s all on a single mission. (Clyde M. Barnes)

23

PISTOL PACKIN MAMA of the 44th Bomb Group was a B-24D-160-C0 Liberator (42-72858) which made a forced landing at Bulltofta Air Field, Malmo, Sweden on 9 April 1944 and was interned for the duration. The mission markings on the Liberator consisted of six shooters and her scoreboard also included a single swastika and three ducks to signify three decoy missions. (Nils-Arne Nilsson)

Hi-Priority Stuff was an F-7B Liberator used in the Southwest Pacific theater and had flown at least twenty-three photographic reconnaissance missions as was shown by the camera symbols on her scoreboard.

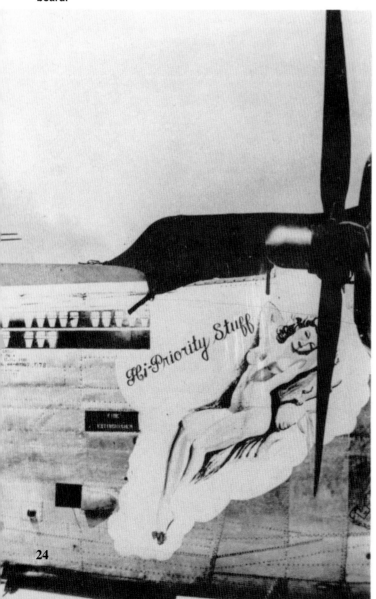

Another PISTOL PACKIN' MAMA, this time from the North African theater, featured a scanty clad cowgirl. The Liberator also used pistols for mission symbols and at least seventeen are visible plus a single air-to-air kill swastika. The name came from a popular song of the period and was one that appeared on a number of different aircraft.

LT William Coleman points to the six enemy kills, portrayed by aircraft silhouettes, claimed by the crew of Jamey. Along with the air-to-air kills, who had flown at least fifty missions, signified by the White bomb symbols. The significance of the lone swastika is unknown.

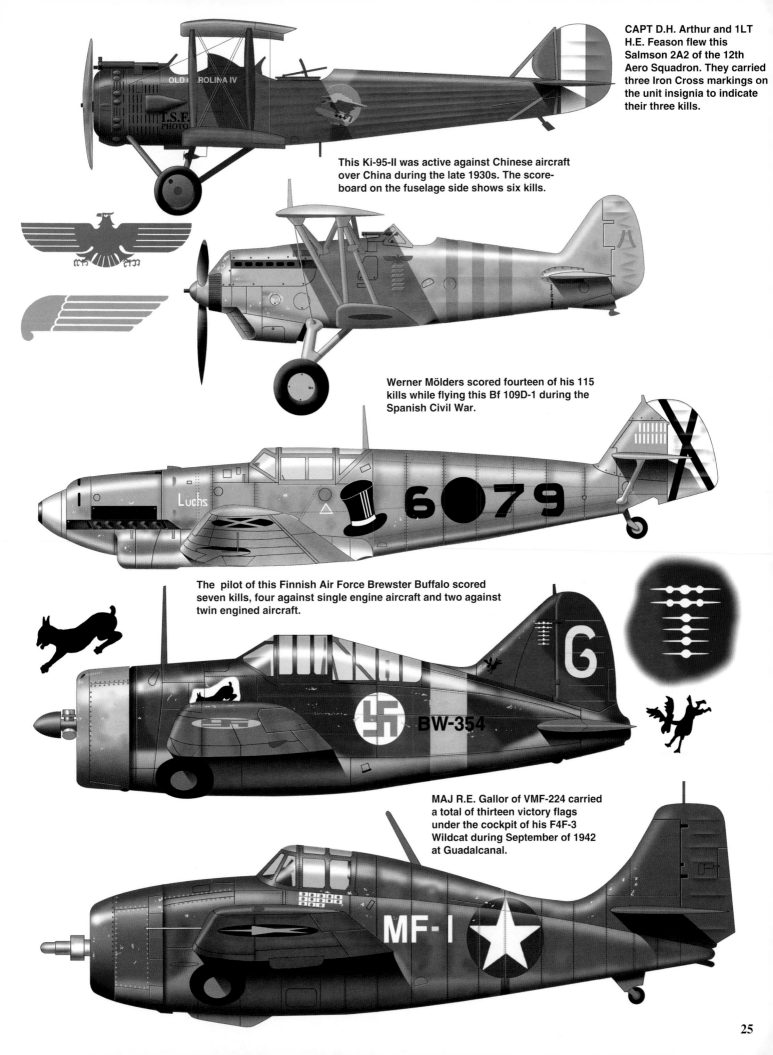

CAPT D.H. Arthur and 1LT H.E. Feason flew this Salmson 2A2 of the 12th Aero Squadron. They carried three Iron Cross markings on the unit insignia to indicate their three kills.

This Ki-95-II was active against Chinese aircraft over China during the late 1930s. The scoreboard on the fuselage side shows six kills.

Werner Mölders scored fourteen of his 115 kills while flying this Bf 109D-1 during the Spanish Civil War.

The pilot of this Finnish Air Force Brewster Buffalo scored seven kills, four against single engine aircraft and two against twin engined aircraft.

MAJ R.E. Gallor of VMF-224 carried a total of thirteen victory flags under the cockpit of his F4F-3 Wildcat during September of 1942 at Guadalcanal.

The 816th Squadron of the 483rd Bomb Group ferried a large number of 5th Army troops between Casa Blanca and Port Lyautey in North Africa and Pisa in Italy. This B-17 flew eighteen such mission in the Summer of 1945 as shown by the Black troop silhouettes. The usual bomb symbols also show that this Fortress had flown its share of combat missions as well. The crewmen are (left to right) SGT Charles K. Foster, LT Victor Prescott and SGT Bernard Boraten. (J.L. Grimm)

The art work on *PHOTO QUEEN* was done by CPL Al Merkling who did a number of other equally interesting paintings on other F-7A Liberators of the 20th Reconnaissance Squadron, 6th Reconnaissance Groups. The QUEEN had flown fourteen missions as indicated by the aerial camera markings but had only been successful on seven as shown by the stars above the cameras. Weather always was a problem on photo missions.

The 530th Squadron of the 380th Bomb Group carried its squadron insignia on the nose of its B-24s. A total of forty-nine mission symbols (four without stars) indicate that this Liberator had four combat recalls but completed forty-five missions and claimed a Zero destroyed.

PATCHED UP PIECE was an F-7A Liberator flown by LT Dave Ecoff of the 67th Photo Reconnaissance Group. On her first mission to cover Morota she developed engine trouble causing him to abort the mission and when both engines on one side went out he made an emergency landing on a partially completed strip on Middleburg. Stars were Recon missions while the clouds were weather sorties.

While this B-24 flown by Lt. William A. Wilson of the 20th Combat Mapping Squadron, 6th Photo Reconnaissance Group in New Guinea did not have a name it certainly had one of the most clever mission scoreboards of the war. Every Army Air Force man knew the meaning of T.S. Cards and this card has been punched four times to indicate completed missions. The aerial camera indicated the type of missions while the star showed they were successful.

A Liberator from the 528th Squadron, 380th Bomb Group, 5th Air Force which was attached to the RAAF most of the war, flew a total of sixty-five missions with only two aborts. She also claimed six enemy aircraft destroyed including three fighters, a pair of twin engine aircraft and a floatplane, which was shown in profile to identify it as a Rufe fighter. The squadron insignia was carried on the nose.

PICCADILY PAM was a Liberator based at Dunkeswell, England where it was attached to the Fleet Air Wing. PAM had ninety V missions and two submarine silhouettes indicating U-boats destroyed. (Via Robert C. Jones)

BLACK JACK of the 98th Bomb Group in North Africa used mule shoes as mission symbols and carried fourteen of them under the name. (98th Bomb Group)

MILADY was a 380th Bomb Group Liberator with eleven completed bombing missions and a lone enemy aircraft destroyed. The air-to-air claim was a most unusual one in that a four engined bomber destroyed a twin engined aircraft.

Northern Star, a B-24D of the 98th Bomb Group, The Pyramiders, was also named Doc as one of the seven dwarfs flight of the 343rd Bomb Squadron. It was flown by LT Glen W. Underwood on the Ploesti raid. Their scoreboard used stars to indicate missions and also the silhouettes of two subs destroyed.

The Wairarapa Wildcat was a P-40M flown by Flight Officer G.B. Fisken of the Royal New Zealand Air Force at Henderson Field, Guadalcanal. The aircraft carried eleven kill markings on the cowling behind the cat.

Josef Wurmheller of JG2 carried a Knight's Cross with sixty kills on the rudder of his Fw-190A-5 along with another twenty kills under the cross.

LT J. Yuri Shtshipov of the 9th IAP carried eight Red star kill markings just forward of his personal marking on his LaGG-3 fighter during 1944.

This P-40E was flown by MAJ P.A. Pokryshev near Leningrad during 1943. He carried a total of fifteen kills above the aircraft side number.

LCOL M.V. Avdeye carried his fifteen victory markings around the national insignia on the fin of his Yak-9D. His personal marking was a diving eagle.

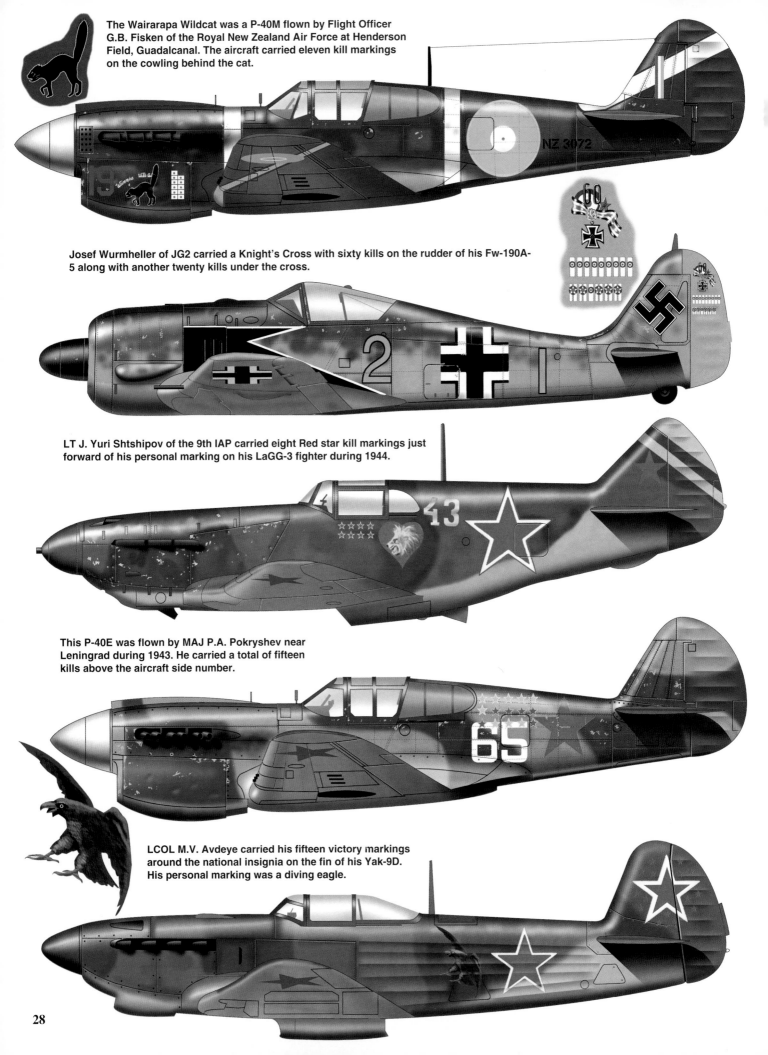

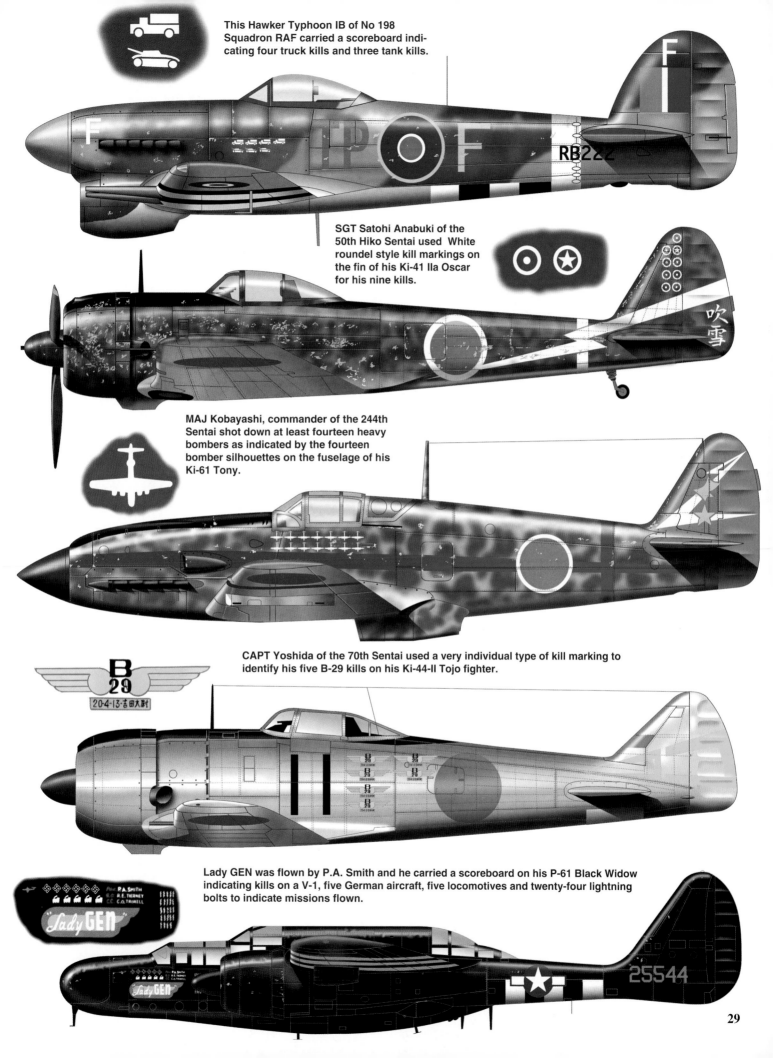

This Hawker Typhoon IB of No 198 Squadron RAF carried a scoreboard indicating four truck kills and three tank kills.

SGT Satohi Anabuki of the 50th Hiko Sentai used White roundel style kill markings on the fin of his Ki-41 IIa Oscar for his nine kills.

MAJ Kobayashi, commander of the 244th Sentai shot down at least fourteen heavy bombers as indicated by the fourteen bomber silhouettes on the fuselage of his Ki-61 Tony.

CAPT Yoshida of the 70th Sentai used a very individual type of kill marking to identify his five B-29 kills on his Ki-44-II Tojo fighter.

Lady GEN was flown by P.A. Smith and he carried a scoreboard on his P-61 Black Widow indicating kills on a V-1, five German aircraft, five locomotives and twenty-four lightning bolts to indicate missions flown.

"Six Bitts", a B-24 Liberator believed to be from the 43rd Bomb Group at Linguyin, Luzon in April of f945 had completed seventy-five missions and claimed five enemy aircraft destroyed. Each bomb had a star above it but in the second row the first six stars have worn off. (James P. Gallagher)

Herky was a B-25D Mitchell (41-30069) of the 501st Bomb Squadron and flew over 125 missions, shot down three enemy aircraft, sank two large ships and six small boats. The aircraft was usually flown by CAPT Henry L. "Knobby" Kroll. (via Larry Hickey)

GONE WITH THE WIND was a B-24D flown by LT George Kubiskie of the Jolly Rogers, the 64th Bomb Squadron of the 43rd Bomb Group. She carried five Japanese flags on a dark Blue scoreboard indicating the number of enemy fighters downed along with 142 missions. The stars above the bomb indicates a completed mission, those without stars were aborts or a weather cancel. The dark bomb above the girl's head may have represented a night mission.

"MITCH THE WITCH" was a B-25 straffer of the 38th Bomb Group at Linsayen, on Luzon during May of 1945. Her scoreboard revealed that she had flown 102 missions without an abort, shot down two enemy aircraft and sank two naval ships, a troop ship and a pair of cargo ships. (J.P. Gallagher)

RITA'S WAGON was a B-25D-5 (41-30055) of the 500th Bomb Squadron Rough Riders and was one of the unit's original group of aircraft. She was flown by 1LT Max H. Mortensen who ended up a LCOL with 109 missions logged and Deputy Commander of the Air Apaches. RITA'S WAGON was named after a friend who died in a crash enroute to the Pacific. It flew over 100 missions, shot down three enemy fighters, sank five freighters and four barges. (M.J. Eppstein via Larry Hickey)

TONDELAYO was named after the Heddy Lamar movie "White Cargo". Later she had the name changed to *Chow Hound* and was one of the Mitchells assigned to the 345th Bomb Group. On 18 October 1943 she was in the unescorted raid on Rabaul and on the return flight engaged in a running fight with fifty Japanese fighters. The other two B-25s in the flight were shot down but SSGT John A. Murphy knocked down five enemy fighters while the crew received credit for four more. The ship on the scoreboard was sunk during the initial attack and was a 6,000 ton freighter. Murphy shot down another Zeke on 12 October to add the 10th flag. (USAAF)

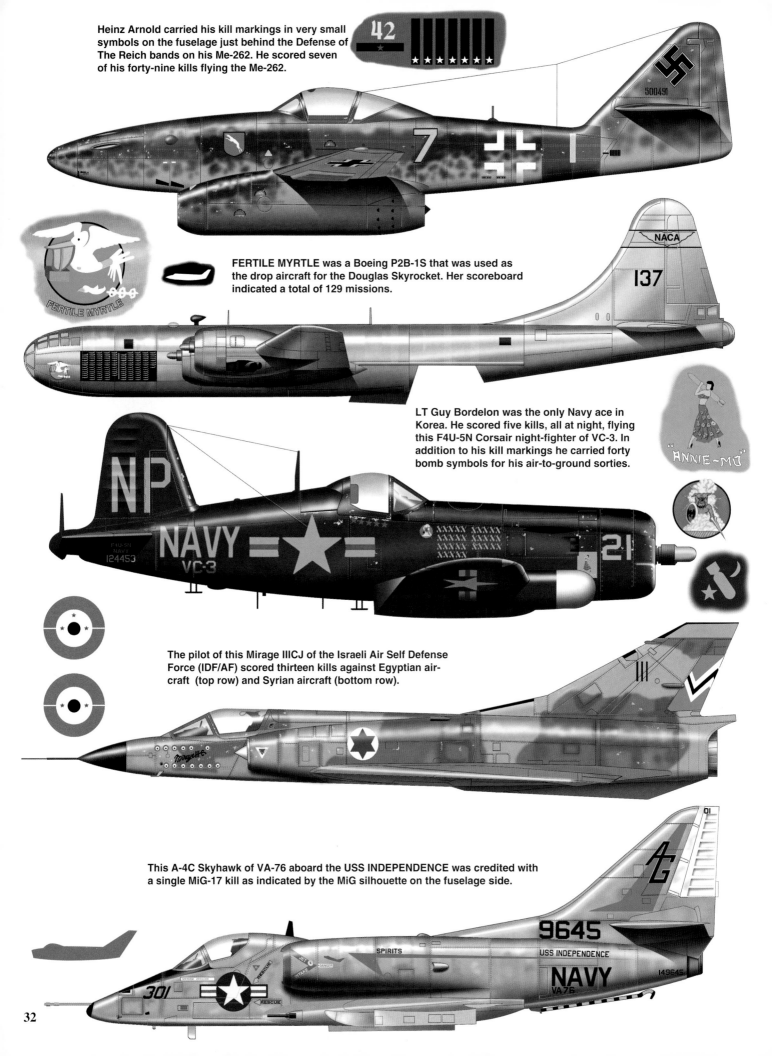

Heinz Arnold carried his kill markings in very small symbols on the fuselage just behind the Defense of The Reich bands on his Me-262. He scored seven of his forty-nine kills flying the Me-262.

FERTILE MYRTLE was a Boeing P2B-1S that was used as the drop aircraft for the Douglas Skyrocket. Her scoreboard indicated a total of 129 missions.

LT Guy Bordelon was the only Navy ace in Korea. He scored five kills, all at night, flying this F4U-5N Corsair night-fighter of VC-3. In addition to his kill markings he carried forty bomb symbols for his air-to-ground sorties.

The pilot of this Mirage IIICJ of the Israeli Air Self Defense Force (IDF/AF) scored thirteen kills against Egyptian aircraft (top row) and Syrian aircraft (bottom row).

This A-4C Skyhawk of VA-76 aboard the USS INDEPENDENCE was credited with a single MiG-17 kill as indicated by the MiG silhouette on the fuselage side.

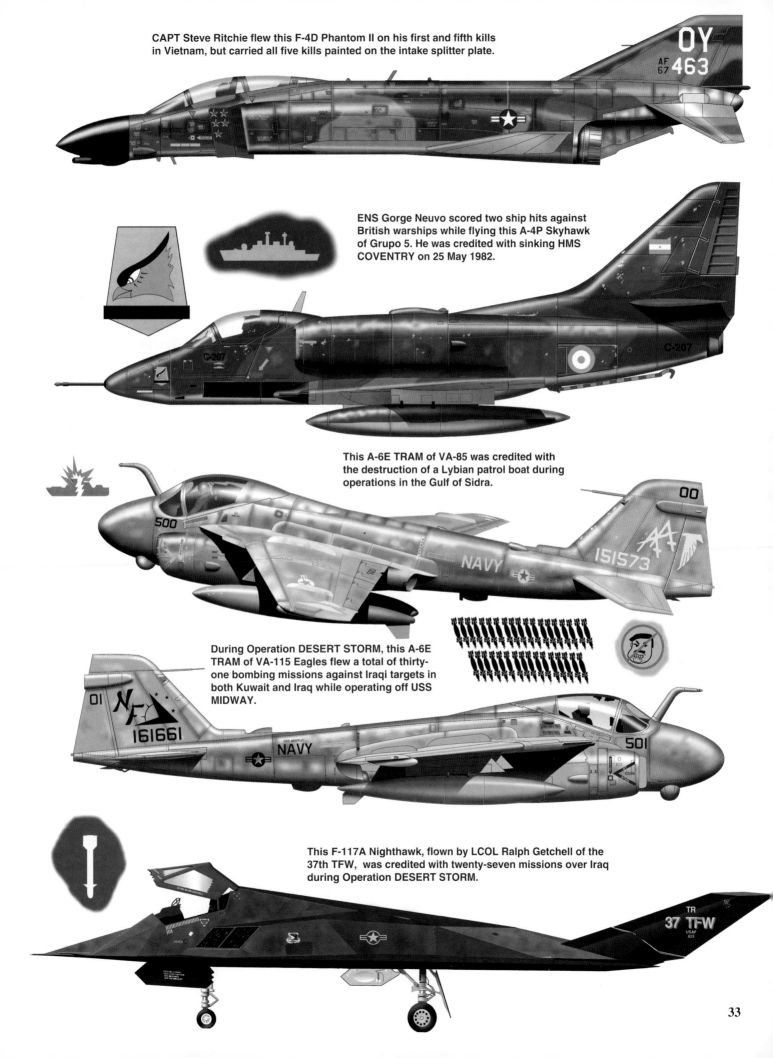

CAPT Steve Ritchie flew this F-4D Phantom II on his first and fifth kills in Vietnam, but carried all five kills painted on the intake splitter plate.

ENS Gorge Neuvo scored two ship hits against British warships while flying this A-4P Skyhawk of Grupo 5. He was credited with sinking HMS COVENTRY on 25 May 1982.

This A-6E TRAM of VA-85 was credited with the destruction of a Lybian patrol boat during operations in the Gulf of Sidra.

During Operation DESERT STORM, this A-6E TRAM of VA-115 Eagles flew a total of thirty-one bombing missions against Iraqi targets in both Kuwait and Iraq while operating off USS MIDWAY.

This F-117A Nighthawk, flown by LCOL Ralph Getchell of the 37th TFW, was credited with twenty-seven missions over Iraq during Operation DESERT STORM.

MY DUCHESS was a B-25-11 (43-36174) which joined the 499th Bomb Squadron of the 345th Bomb Group on 25 October 1944 and was assigned to 1LT Newton E. Wiley. Before being written off on 12 July 1945 in a landing accident at Clark field, DUCHESS put in twenty-six missions and sank eight enemy ships. (M.J. Eppstein via Larry Hickey)

DESERT WARRIOR of the 12th Bomb Group Earthquakers, was a B-25 Mitchell that had flown seventy-three missions, dropped seventy tons of bombs and claimed three enemy aircraft destroyed while flying 199 combat hours. This earned it the right to be sent back to the States on a war weary War Bond Tour. (USAAF)

Old Schenley was a B-25D-30 (43-3491) of the 501st Squadron but was usually flown by Group Headquarters Officers including COL Clinton U. True and LCOL Chester A. Coltharp. SGT Watt was the crew chief. While with the Air Apaches it flew twenty-eight missions as indicated by the rows of smaller bottles of Old Schenley used as mission markers. The aircraft was based at Eagle Farm Air Field near Brisbane, Australia during September of 1944. (J.C. Hanna via Larry Hickey)

This B-25J Mitchell of the Royal Netherlands Air Force has two ships silhouettes along with forty-two White bombs. In addition the top turret gunner had two Japanese flags under his turret for the two enemy aircraft he has claimed as destroyed. (Steve Birdsall)

Wash's Tub earned this citation painted on the fuselage while serving with the Liberandos. The B-24D Liberator was one of the original Halpro aircraft and flew seventy-three missions, dropped 219 tons of bombs, shot down twenty-two enemy fighters and sank five enemy ships. It flew close to 100,000 miles and had a total of 551.35 combat hours while with the 376th Bomb Group in Africa. (James V. Crow)

MELBA JEANE's crew picked an easy way to keep their score totalled up without a lot of work. They simply applied a large thermometer with room to move the Red line up scale as they flew missions but when it hit 100 and ran out of space they decided to add small bombs with the Red mercury line to indicate a successful mission. The aircrat served with the 17th Bomb Group. (V.C. Tannehill)

"Saturday Nite" was a B-25D-5 (41-30079) of the 500th Bomb Squadron. It joined the Apaches at Savannah, Georgia in March of 1943 and originally it carried a large bee with a bomb on its back on both sides of the fuselage. Later a large tigers head was painted on the entire nose like the bat heads used by the 499th Bats Outa Hell Squadron. On 17 September 1943, SSGT Charlie Brown shot down a Zeke on a leaflet mission for the Groups first aerial kill, winning the Air Medal and a Purple Heart for the feat. PVT J.R. Weimer later bagged another Zeke. The crew earned three Purple Hearts and flew over fifty-five missions. (J.C. Hanna via Larry Hickey)

DIANA'S DEMON was a B-26 of an unknown unit that followed the standard practice of simply using a bomb as a symbol for each mission flown. There are ten bombs with only two of them lacking stars above them. It was a practice to use a star to indicate a lead mission, although some crews used stars to indicate a completed mission, while no star meant an abort or an inability to hit the target due to weather conditions.

Paradise Isle was an F-80C Shooting Star of the 25th Fighter Interceptor Squadron, 51st Fighter Wing at Suwon Korea during 1951-52. Her scoreboard indicated that she flew at least 106 bombing missions. (CAPT B. V Moore II)

MAJ F. C. "Boots" Blesse flew this F-86F Sabre of the 334th Fighter Interceptor Squadron, 4th Fighter Group and gained a total of ten victories as indicated by the ten Red stars carried under the cockpit. Today the aircraft is on display at the Champlin Fighter Museum in Mesa, Arizona. (COL J. Ward Boyce)

This F-4D Phantom II was flown by CAPT Steve Ritchie of the 555th Tactical Fighter Squadron, 432rd Tactical Fighter Wing out of Udorn, Thailand during 1972. Ritchie was the first USAF ace in Vietnam scoring a total of five kills represented by the five Red stars on the intake splitter plate. (David W. Menard)

This F-4B Phantom II of VF-161 Chargers aboard USS MIDWAY during January of 1973 carried a MiG-17 silhouette on the splitter plate with a White 5 in the center to represent the five MiG kills scored by the squadron during the Vietnam war. The squadron later scored a sixth MiG kill (the last Navy MiG kill of the war). (Bernie Moore)

This A-4E Skyhawk of the Navy Fighter Weapons School (Topgun) was flown by LT Winston Copeland (aka MAD DOG) and carried a Red star on the name plate to indicate that LT Copeland was a MiG killer (1972 aboard USS CORAL SEA). It is a common practice for pilots to carry over their kills from one aircraft to another. This Skyhawk as later transferred to the Israeli Air Force during 1973 to make up for combat losses in the Yom Kipper War. (CAPT Bernard V. Moore II)

A Lockheed AC-130A (16505) Specter gunship on the ramp at Ubon Royal Thai Air Base, Thailand during 1968. The aircraft carried mission markings in the form of Black Vulcan cannons on the fuselage side just in front of the Vulcan cannon ports. The unit insignia was that of the 16th Special Operations Squadron. (Larry Davis)

CDR Mazurczak of VP-60 carried Black silhouettes of submarines on the nose of his P-3C Orion to indicate successful Anti-Submarine Warfare detection sorties. The different silhouettes identified the various types of submarines found and identified by the crew. The aircraft also carried the commander's call sign KING COBRA on the nose in Black. (Author)

MAJ R. McCullough painted three White tree silhouettes on the nose of his A-7D of the 112th Tactical Fighter Group, Pennsylvania Air National Guard for the three evergreen trees he clipped while on a low level practice bombing mission. The aircraft was named *Passionate Pruner.* (Dana Bell)

This record breaking Lockheed YF-12A was flown by COL Robert L. Stephens and his rear seater, LCOL Daniel Andre for an average speed of 2,069 mph (Mach 3.17). It also set two other records over 500 and 1,000 km courses (1,698 and 1, 643 mph respectively. The aircraft carried three White YF-12A silhouettes under the cockpit with the record information on each during May of 1969. (David Musikoff)

This B-52G Stratofortress of the Air Force Systems Command at Edwards Air Force Base during May of 1980 carried ten Black cruise missile silhouettes on the fuselage under the aircraft side number to indicate the number of successful missile launches. The aircraft carried both the SAC and Systems Command insignias on the fuselage under the cockpit. (Dick Starinchak via Larry Davis)

The FLYING SUBMARINE was a Ryan AQM-3Q target drone that was launched by a DC-130. After each sortie, the drone was painted with a White mission marking on the side. Out of the twenty-three sorties shown, the aircraft went into the water (markings without parachutes) five different times, earning it the name it carried on the fuselage in White. (Author)

The crew of this 17th Bomb Group B-26C-1 Marauder apparently elected to save the ground crew artists a lot of trouble by using a single large bomb to indicate the completion of their first 100 missions and then added three more small bombs to round out their grand total. (V. C. Tannehill)

This Martin B-26 Marauder of the 17th Bomb Group used Red apples as mission markers hoping that "an apple a day" would keep the Flight Surgeon away. Following the forty-fourth Red apple were the words "Fini La Guerre" in Black. (V.C. Tannehill)

SHANGHAI LIL Rides Again carries symbols on her scoreboard indicating that she had flown three photo reconnaissance missions, seven bombing missions, and had flown the "hump" eight times. During this period, two of her crew suffered wounds and won Purple Hearts (first and fifth bombing missions). (Larry Davis)

Joltin' Josie, The Pacific Pioneer was the first B-29 to arrive in the Marianas, landing on Isley Field on 12 October 1944. She served as a member of the 498th Group and her scoreboard showed twenty-three completed missions. The ten Japanese flags indicated five enemy aircraft destroyed and five shared kills are indicated by the other five which have only half the meatball painted in Red.

NIGHTMARE had one of the more unusual nose art paintings. She carried nine camels and ten bombs on her scoreboard. The camels represented missions over the "hump" from India to China.

KAGU TSUCHI, THE SCOURGE OF THE FIRE GOD was the group insignia used by the 40th Bomb Group based at West Field, Tinian. This B-29-A-15BN Superfortress (44-61746) of the 45th Bomb Squadron carried three weather reconnaissance mission symbols in the form of Red weather vanes.

MAN O WAR was named for a Kentucky Derby winner. The B-29-60-BA Superfortress (44-84076) carried a scoreboard with eight Black bomb symbols and thirteen camels (for "hump" mission). The bomber was preserved and is on display at Offutt Air Force Base, the headquarters for SAC. (Art Krieger)

"VIRGIN SQUAW" was a B-29 Superfortress of the 3rd Bomb Group had a unique scoreboard where each Black bomb stood for five missions (and was marked with a White Roman numeral V). This practice saved both a lot of time and paint. (P. Yant)

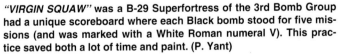

EL PAJARO carried a diving bird on a cherry bomb symbol and the date of each mission completed. The scoreboard on the B-29 carried a total of thirty missions with circles in place for another eight. The Superfortress was Natural Metal with Flat Black undersurfaces. (Kohn)

MAJ R. Pauly flew the NEW ORLEANS LADY, an A-10A Thunderbolt II.The scoreboard on his A-10 shows that during Operation DESERT STORM, MAJ Pauly destroyed seven tanks, four APCs, seven guns, three radars and eight trucks. (Dana Bell)

The CITY OF SUMPTER, an A-10A of the 21st Tactical Fighter Squadron carried a scoreboard that included five radars, 1 mobile missile launcher, nineteen guns, five tanks, fourteen armored cars/APCs, one aircraft, one helicopter and fifteen trucks. (Dana Bell)

COL R. N. Parsons shot down an Su-20/22 in GULF SPIRIT on 7 February 1991 while CAPT A.R. Murphy shot down two SU-22s while flying the SPIRIT later on that same day. All were destroyed with AIM-7 Sparrow missiles.(R. F. Dorr)

Marine Corps CAPT Lixxekin flew a total of forty-six bombing missions during Operation DESERT STORM in this AV-8B Harrier of VFMA-231.

The Black mission markings on this RAF Jaguar include general purpose bombs, missiles, rockets and cluster bombs. The lettering on each gave the weight and number of bombs carried on each mission(Lars Knudsen)

THUMPER, a B-29-40-BW (42-24623) was having the results of its fifteenth mission added to its scoreboard. The crew claimed six enemy aircraft destroyed on that mission. Eventually at least twenty-five little Thumpers were carried to denote the total missions. Thumpers were carrying a total of fourteen flags when the twenty-fifth mission was completed. Each bomb carried the name of the target.

The *ENOLA GAY* of the 509th Composite Group was a B-29-45-MO Superfortress (44-86292). Her scoreboard had five "Fat Man" atomic bomb mission symbols which were unique to this group and represented missions on which five ton high explosive bombs were dropped in preparation for the Atomic Bomb drop.

CAMEL CARAVAN, a B-29 (42-6333)of the 793rd Bomb Squadron, 468th Bomb Group was converted to the tanker configuration on 21 May 1944. During its career she flew forty-seven missions over the "hump" as indicated by the Black camels on the nose. Declared war weary, she returned to the States on 26 November 1944. (Via John Campbell)

This De HavillandMosquito Mk XVI (now in the USAF Museum Collection) carried twenty-four Red lightning flashes each piercing a White cloud to indicate weather reconnaissance sorties over the Continent. It carries the markings of the 653rd Squadron, 25th Bomb Group stationed at Watton during 1944. Pilots came from the P-38 equipped 50th Fighter Squadron. (USAF Museum)

Naval Aircraft

Due to the nature of carrier aviation, it was almost impossible to assign a pilot a specific aircraft within the squadron or air group. There might be rare exceptions, but naval pilots usually flew the aircraft they were assigned on a daily basis, and that depended on maintenance, how the aircraft were spotted on the deck and many other factors. As a result, pilots would put their name and scoreboard on one aircraft but that aircraft may not have been the one they scored the kill or flew the mission in.

In the case of fighters, aircraft returning from a mission were spotted on deck as they landed, so when the next mission came up, other pilots would probably fly these aircraft.

Other than scoreboards, personal markings on Naval aircraft are rare. Often, the same aircraft would be repainted with the names and kills of aces for press releases and their actual aircraft did not carry these markings.

(Above and left) This Grumman F6F-3 Hellcat, side number 12 of Fighter Squadron Thirty-One (VF-31) aboard USS CABOT was used by each of these three aces for publicity photos. The aircraft was repainted with each man's scoreboard along with nine White bomb symbols and the unit markings for the photo shoots. LTs Arthur R Hawkins and John L. Worth each had fourteen kills, while LT Cornelious N. Nooy had fifteen (eighteen by war's end). Later Nooy and Hawkins flew tours aboard USS BELLEAU WOOD. (R.M. Hill)

CDR David S. McCampbell of VF-15 aboard the USS ESSEX was the top scoring ace in the Navy with a total of thirty-four air-to-air kills and twenty additional ground kills (the Navy did not grant credit for ground kills). McCampbell flew serveral F6Fs (F6F-3s and F6F-5s) all named Minzi (I thru III). He was one of the few to have an individual aircraft assigned to him because of his status as air group commander. His aircraft was always spotted so that it would be available to him. He was awarded the Medal of Honor for scoring seven kills on a single mission. Minzi III's scoreboard has twenty-one kills on the fuselage under the cockpit. (R.M. Hill)

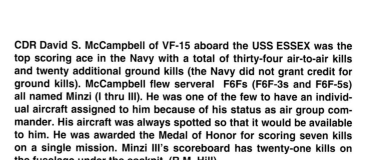

LT Alexander Vraciu of VF-16 was tied for third place among the Navy's top scoring aces. He had a total of sixteen victories (although there are nineteen Japanese flags on his F6F. He served aboard USS INDEPENDENCE and USS LEXINGTON during the Summer of 1944.

LT Ira C. Kepford finished the war with a total of seventeen confirmed kills. He was land based in the Solomons with VF-17 and had his own aircraft, number 29, assigned to him which carried his scoreboard on the fuselage side under the cockpit. His F4U-1D Corsair was probably one of the best known of the war. (USN)

Other WW II U.S./ALLIED AIRCRAFT

Other aircraft types besides fighters and bombers also carried mission markings. Transports, rescue aircraft and even trainers carried mission markings.

Allied aircraft based with or operating along side U.S. Forces also carried these types of markings to record the accomplishments of their crews.

(Right) This OA-10 Catalina Dumbo Army Air Force air-sea rescue aircraft carried a total of eighty-one search and rescue missions which were indicated by life rafts. The stars indicate that these missions resulted in a life saving rescue. (R. M. Hill)

Native canoes surround this Consolidated OA-10A Catalina rescue aircraft. These aircraft were called Dumbos by their crews. Although carrying Navy colors, these aircraft were flown by the USAAF. This Dumbo of the 2nd Emergency Rescue Squadron was based at Middleburg Island. This aircraft was built by Vickers in Canada. (USAF)

This beached PBY-5A Dumbo air-sea rescue aircaft sports a scoreboard with forty mission symbols and five stars for successful rescues. The Red Cross vehicle was on hand with coffee and donuts for the tired crew after returning from a successful rescue mission. (R.M. Hill)

JERRY GEE was a PBY-5A of VP-81 the Black Cat Squadron at Guadalcanal in June of 1944. The Catalinas had a crew of four officers and seven enlisted men. The PBY had at least twenty-nine missions to its credit and had sank seven barges. (F.C. Dickey Jr.)

(Above & Below) This RAAF Supermarine Walrus (believed to be from No 9 Squadron, RAAF) was stationed at Cape Gloucester, New Britain during June of 1944 and was named *Rescue's Angel*. Its markings included fourteen stretchers and six life rafts. On the starboard side of the fuselage it sported a Mermaid just to the rear of the name. The life raft markings are located behind the upper row of stretchers in a row of five plus one below it. (J P Gallagher)

(Below and Right) The PIONEER MUSTANG SKYLINER belonged to the 354th Fighter Group and was used as a squadron transport. It is unclear if the Black cross symbols were the total kills of the entire Group or had another meaning. COL George R. Bickell was commander of the group from April of 1944 until May of 1945. The legend on the door stated that there were 950 "Kaput Krauts". (J.V. Crow)

45

Great Britain/ Commonwealth

The RAF high command frowned on any type of flamboyant personal or victory markings, especially on fighter types. They felt that an unusually marked or decorated aircraft would be given priority and extra attention by enemy fighters. The few Spitfires and Hurricanes aces that carried kill markings kept them relatively small and less obvious and in many cases were flown by pilots from Commonwealth countries and in theaters other than in Great Britain itself.

The pilots attached to the RAF from the British colonies were much more inclined to use nose art of the girlie or pinup type, apply names to their aircraft and use victory and mission marking symbols.

Bomber crews were given a bit more leeway, since most flew by night and were allowed the full range of personal and squadron or group markings. These crews came up with numerous personal mission symbols such as ice cream cones for easy missions, windmills indicated drops of food or agents into the Netherlands, full moons for night sorties and much more.

MAJ Z. Krasnodesbski of No 303 Squadron (Kosciuszko Squadron) in the cockpit of his Spitfire. He carried the No 303 Squadron insignia over his eleven victory crosses. The Iron Cross above the kill markings was unexplained as are the RAF sergeant stripes on his arm. (Art Krieger)

(Right) This Spitfire was flown by the Australian ace, Cleve R. Caldwell. His scoreboard had a total of twenty-two German, three and half Italian and seven Japanese kills. (Alan Shader)

CAPT E. Horbaczewski, commander of No 315 Squadron shot down sixteen and a half enemy aircraft as shown on the scoreboard painted on his Mustang Mk III in August of 1944, shortly before he was killed in action.The squadron was staffed by Polish pilots and carried the Polish national insignia on the nose. The aircraft also carried twenty-six bomb symbols. The four kills with V-1 silhouettes signify the destruction of four of these flying bombs. (via Bill Hess and Brian Shadbolt)

(Above and below) Li'l Henry (a British comic strip character) was the mascot of this Lancaster Mk I of No 463 Squadron that took part in the final Lancaster raid of the war on 26 April 1945. It was part of an eighty-eight aircraft mission to bomb the oil refinery at Vallo near Tonsberg, Norway. A German night fighter attacked the Lancaster and was shot down during the engagement, however, the bomber was crippled and several crew members wounded so the aircraft landed in Sweden. The mission markings on the nose were in the form of slingshots (like that carried by the comic character). She was the 20th Lancaster to be forced down in Sweden and was eventually scrapped. (Bo Widfeld via N.A. Nilsson)

This Vickers Wellington of No l08 Squadron was based at Landing Ground 237 somewhere in the Middle East. She had completed eighty-seven missions (or operations as the British called them) as of 12 August 1942. The mission markings were minature *Saint* figures. *The Saint* was a popular fictional character in British mystery books at the time. (R.J. Souter via R.C. Jones)

Itzabugar was a Wellington of No 108 Squadron at Landing Ground 237 in the Middle East which was reportedly the first in that squadron to use mission markings. She flew forty-five missions as shown by the White bombs on the nose. (R.J. Soutar via R.C. Jones)

LUCIFER was a B-24J of No 335 Squadron RAF based in Burma. She carried thirty White bombs on a Black scoreboard indicating night missions and thirteen White bombs for daylight operations. The small aircraft silhouette may have been a part of the crews emblem or it may have represented a kill by the nose gunner. (Robert C. Jones)

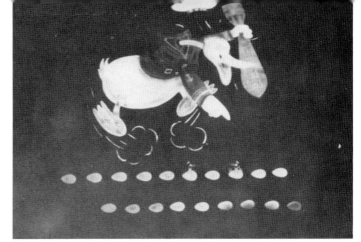

The British also used Disney characters. Here Donald Duck was holding a bomb and throwing his usual fit as two of his eggs hatched, indicating two unsatisfactory operations. The good eggs represented eighteen successful missions flown by this Vickers Wellington IC (JN-D) of No 150 Squadron based at Snaith. (J.L. Bullen via R.C. Jones)

(Left) The motto of the crew of this Beaufighter was simple: Wine,Women and Song. The aircraft was based in the Western Desert and its scoreboard shows at least two kills. (Jerry Scutts)

This crashed Handley Page Halifax of No 434 (Bluenose) Squadron, Royal Canadian Air Force, coded WL-M (serial LW 171) used beer bottles as their mission marker for completed missions. They also carried a single swastika kill marking and a lone beer stein which stood for a leaflet drop. The name appears to be *Yes Mullican*. (Bryan Philpott via R.C. Jones)

This B-24J of No 223 Squadron, 100 Group, RAF Bomber Command, which was a bomber support unit, flew radio counter-measures sorties as indicated by the Red lightning flash mission symbols. Coded GS-J with the serial T5520, the Liberator had the nose turret faired over. The crew included J. Adams, I. Leslie, A. Alnutt, J. Maunsell, D. Townsend, E. Laraway, T. Tucker, E. Manners and J. Tucker. (R.C. Jones)

SOVIET AIR FORCE

Victory symbols were used on a number of different fighter aircraft such as the LaGG-3, La-5NF, Yak-l, Yak-7, and Yak-9. In addition it was common to see victory marking on Lend-Lease P-39s, P-40s and Hurricane Mk IIs. With but two exceptions the victory or kill markings consisted of Soviet stars. The two exceptions were the Free French Group known as the Normandie-Nieman and a female Russian ace named Lily Litvak, known as the "White Rose of Stalingrad." The French flew Yaks that carried small Balkenkreuzes for kill symbols, while Lily used small White roses to denote the twelve Nazi aircraft she destroyed in combat.

Since all Soviet kill markings were the basic Soviet star, variations were naturally limited to outlines used as borders of the star, in the color of the star itself, and in the placement of these symbols on the aircraft itself. When medals were earned by the pilot, he had the medal painted on his plane. The majority of the stars were red, however, one ace who used white stars also carried (in Russian) the legend "Death to Fascists" on the fuselage just to the rear of his scoreboard

For the most part P-40 pilots carried their stars behind the cockpit on the turtle deck. P-39 pilots used several spots including: on the nose, on the cockpit door, above the exhaust stacks, and just in front of the door. CAPT Vasili S. Adonkln who flew a Hurricane Mk II with the side number 80 carried his ten stars behind the national insignia in a single row extending almost to the tail. Yak and LaGG pilots mostly carried their kill markings under the cockpit on the fuselage, on the fin and rudder, or just to the rear of the cockpit on the turtle deck. Personal emblems were permitted and these included eagles, serpents, stylized shooting stars, shark's teeth, leopards, lions, and so on. LT Litvak used a large White rose as her personal marking in addition to the smaller kill

CAPT Grigori A. Rechkalov, a squadron commander in the 16 Gv. IAP talks with pilots of his unit in front of his Bell P-39N Airacobra.The fighter carried fifty-five Red stars, outlined in White, on the nose. He won his second Hero of the Soviet Union award flying this aircraft. His total was fifty-six kills and five shared victories in a total of 122 missions.

marking roses. Many aircraft carried patriotic slogans, threats to the enemy, and public funded aircraft usually carried the sponsoring groups name or names. Certain Guards squadrons carried their unit badges on the fuselage.

Some of the inscriptions mentioned include:. "Eskadrilya Valeri Chkalov" (Valeri Chkalov Squadron) which was named after a famous test pilot, ""Za Vasek i Zhora" (For Vasek and Zhora), "Za Brata Shota" (For Brother Shota), "Za Staline" (For Stalin), "Za Rodlinu" (For the Fatherland) and "Za Partil Bolshevikov" (For the Party of the Bolsheviks).

There were a number of four line inscriptions that pretty well filled the entire fuselage and they all ran pretty much the same, such as "To the Defenders of the Stalingrad Front from the workers of the Krasnoyarsk District in the Saratow Area". Others carried similar inscriptions with the donors names, factory, areas and to whom the plane was dedicated or given.

Colored spinners, fuselage and tail bands, lightning flashes or arrows running the length of the fuselage and chevrons served as identification markings.

Senior LT Mihail Baranov, Hero of the Soviet Union, waves from the cockpit of his Yak-1. The aircraft carried an individual slogan and a scoreboard of twenty-four Red stars on the fuselage (his final score was twenty-seven. (Via Hans-Heiri Stapfer)

A flight of Yak-9D fighters led by LCOL Mikhail V. Avdeyev who was an ace with fifteen kills. Avdeyev was commander of the 6 Gv. IAP, Black Sea Fleet. The Guards emblem and Order of the Red Banner were carried on the nose and the six kills were on the fin placed on each side of the upper point of the Red Star. He later flew a Yak-9D with an eagle on the fuselage where the number had been. This aircraft carried all fifteen stars on the fin. (Via Hans-Heiri Stapfer)

CAPT B. I. Chepinoga (Tshepinoga), commander of 508th IAP shows off his seven medals and the twenty-four victory symbols that earned him these medals. The stars were Red with a thin Yellow outline. Chepinoga was made a Hero of the Soviet Union on 26 October 1944. He flew a Bell P-39Q Airacobra for all of his missions. (Via Klaus Niska)

Senior LT Nicolai Kuznetzov being greeted by his squadron mates after adding another two enemy aircraft to his credit, running his total to up to fourteen kills. His Curtiss P-40K Kittyhawk carries twelve White stars on the fuselage side in front of the aircraft side number.

(Right) This unidentified pilot had his scoreboard of eight stars arranged around the side number of his P-39. He also had a photo of a young lady and a Red lightning bolt on the fuselage side. (Pavel Zaporozhets)

MAJ Ivan N. Kozhedub of the l76th Guards Regiment, a three time Hero of the Soviet Union, had sixty-two victories. This La5-FN now hangs in the Frunze Central House of Aviation. His last victory was in an overall White aircraft with a Red nose and Blue fin and rudder.

This Bell P-63 at Duxford, England has been restored in the markings of MAJ V. F. Sirotin who was vice commander of the 17th IAP. His victory markings were carried on both doors of his Kingcobra and his personal emblem, an eagle, was on both sides of the nose. He had a total of twenty Red stars with thin White outlines (on his actual aircraft the nineteen were not outlined). (Lars Kundsen)

This Yak-3 was flown by S/L Rene Challe of the 1st Escadrille, Normandie-Neimen French Regiment in Russia. Rene was credited with eight kills as indicated by the eight crosses behind the cockpit of his Yak. Only the French were allowed to use the German crosses as victory symbols in Russia and the kill markings were displayed on both sides. (Via Hans-Heiri Stapfer-E.C.P. Armees)

S/L Roger Marchi in the cockpit of his Yak-3 White 4. He was credited with thirteen German kills during his tour with the Normandie-Niemen Regiment. Apparently , the French applied the victory markings in the same positions on the Yak-3s in French service. (E.C.P. Armees via Hans-Heiri Stapfer)

Yak-3s of the Normandie-Nieman Regiment on the grass at Stuttgart, Germany, enroute to LeBourget, France in June of 1945. As a tribute to their efforts the Russians presented the aircraft to the pilots. These were from the 1st Escadrille commanded by Rene Challe. The Free French Cross of Lorraine has been painted on the fin. (E.C.P. Armees via Hans-Heiri Stapfer)

JAPAN

Victory or kill markings were commonly used in the Japanese Army Air Force and were popular in the Japanese Navy Air Force as well. Unlike most other air forces, the Japanese credited the victory to the aircraft rather than the pilot who scored it, therefore a fighter with a very large number of victory symbols was not necessarily that of a top ace since the kills may have been made by several different pilots flying the same aircraft. The USAF adopted this system during the Vietnam War and used it on Phantoms. The U.S. Navy also used a similar system on its aircraft.

As in any system, exceptions existed. Japanese pilots of higher rank or unit leaders often had their own personal aircraft and all kill markings appearing on that aircraft reflected the score of that pilot. In some cases, where aircraft were used by more than one pilot, an individual pilot would have his personal Kanji (marking) alongside the kills he scored.

Both Army and Navy aircraft commonly carried these symbols on the left side only, under the cockpit. Multiplace aircraft usually placed them on the rear fuselage and in a few cases they were put on the fin or rudder. As different pilots had their own personal victory symbols, several different types might appear on the same aircraft.

Some of the different types of symbols used included birds, bird wings, cherry blossoms, Chrysanthemums, daisies, stars and silhouettes of enemy aircraft. Stylized versions of all of these were also used and the mums were never exact replicas of the Chrysanthemums that were sacred to the Emperor. In the cases of aircraft symbols were mostly plan views and fairly accurate representations of the type of enemy aircraft claimed as destroyed.

The star originally was used during the Nomamhan Incident and remained in use from 1938 until 1942. Initially, they were Red Stars but later, when a darker camouflage was applied to the aircraft, they were painted White or Yellow.

The Cherry Blossom was in use from 1938 until the end of the war. Cherry Blossoms were used in two forms, either a solid color or a sten-

This Mitsubishi A6M2 Type O Navy fighter Model 21 carried the tail number of X-183 and was flown by the 3rd Air Corps based at Kendari in the Celebes during 1942. Eleven cherry blossom victory symbols are carried on the fin. (Via Al Makiel)

ciled outline. The solid color type had interior detailing in Black but the detail was omitted if the claim was either a probable or a shared kill. Solid color blossoms were sometimes outlined in Pink or Yellow. Mums or daisies were pretty much treated in the same manner so far as colors were concerned.

As mentioned previously, the plan view silhouettes usually took the form of the enemy aircraft shot down. A large X of two crossed arrows indicated a confirmed kill, a single arrow meant a shared victory or a probable. In some cases a bar was used instead of the arrow. Bolts of lightning through the silhouette indicated a kill. On most aircraft the plan view was stenciled in a nose down position and the arrows also pointed down to indicate the enemy was shot down.

While there may have been symbols to indicate missions flown by bombers, none have been turned up in our research.

Regimental commander Teruhiko Kobayashi of the 224th Fighter Regiment, Home Island Defense Sentai poses in front of his Ki-61-I-Kai Tony fighter. He had a total of twenty kills before the end of the war. (M. Toda)

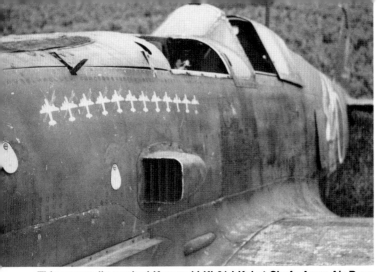

This unusually marked Kawasaki Ki-61-I-Kai at Chofu Army Air Base near Tokyo in September of 1945 had a Green shamrock outlined in White just ahead of the national marking. Twelve White B-29 silhouettes with a Red comet like streak across each indicated twelve kills. (James P. Gallagher)

This Kawasaki Ki-61 Hein (Tony) was captured after the war. The aircraft still carried its original camouflage and had two White B-29 kill silhouettes under the cockpit. (James V. Crow)

Germany

During the Second World War, the Luftwaffe, while favoring kill markings, kept them relatively simple and in one location as a rule. Most consisted of just a bar or long rectangular marking which was displayed on the rudder. These ranged from a solid White or Black bar to an oversized bar that included the number of kills represented. Later totals were painted on the rudder, followed by bars to indicate the number of victories gained after that point. Individual variations were used by pilots to indicate the nationality of the aircraft downed, others added the date of the kill, another variation was the type by name, while still others

marked the date and area where the combat took place. The more interesting markings included the medal won by the pilot along with his total score at the time of the award. By adding an eagle, oak leafs, swords, and the medal with its ribbon, some highly colorful and individual score markings were created. Pilots who fought in the Condor Legion of the Spanish Civil War carried a simple White bar on the rudder for each kill scored.

It was the bomber groups that really went all out to record their accomplishments on the fins or rudders of their aircraft. Those that sank Allied shipping painted accurate ship type silhouettes on their aircraft. Some carried the name of the ship or type, others the date of sinking and/or location the attack took place. Some carried paintings of the type of industrial targets destroyed such as factories, oil supplies, and even barrage balloons, or civilian workers. A Henschel on the Russian front had eight tanks in a vertical row on the rudder.

(Left) The rudder of Heinrich Klopper's Bf-109G of 7 III/JG 1, who made a crash landing at Eelde, Holland during mid-1943 shows that his score was ninety-one kills at that time. He later added three more to finish with a total of ninety-four kills. The Black bars with the diagonal line (nos.3 and 15) represent twin engine aircraft, while the ones with two diagonals represented four engined aircraft, all American bombers. Klopper was lost over the Zuider Zee on 29 September 1943. (James V. Crow)

An unidentified Bf-109 carries standard victory bar type markings that are interesting in that the first ten at the top lack any nationality markings while all the others bear roundel above the bar and what appears to be dates under the roundels. (James V. Crow)

Oblt Siegfried Schnell, Staffelkapitan of 9 III/JG2 admires his score of at least forty-seven victories in the Spring of 1943 in France. He had a total of eighty-seven kills in the West before being posted to Russia where he brought his score up to ninety-three before being shot down and killed on 25 February 1944. Schnell favored showing the nationality of his kills in the center of his White victory bars. (James V. Crow)

The Bf-109E of ZI/JG 27 in the foreground carries a rare victory bar as its first kill, that of a Polish aircraft. The other fourteen are all Royal Air Force types. In the Spring of 1941 these Bf-109s were based at Strimatal, Bulgaria. The Bf-109 in the middle is that of Gruppenkommander Hapt Wolfgang Lippert. (James V. Crow)

Ober Leutnant Otto Schuz of II/JG 27 in North Africa carried forty-four kills on the rudder of his Bf-109F-4/Trop during February of 1942. He was killed in action on 17 June 1942 and had a total of fifty-one victories at the time of his death. His 7th, 8th, and 9th kills were Russian aircraft. (James V. Crow)

Oblt Hans Schopper, Staffelkapitan of 1 I/JG4 had thirty-four Black victory bars on the rudder of his Bf-109G in Rumania during 1943. The first four victories were Royal Air Force aircraft and the balance were Russian. He had the national identification markings applied under each bar. (James V. Crow)

Ober Leutnant Siegfried Lemke of 1 I/JG 2 shows off his Knights Cross and forty-eight plain White victory bar markings. He went on to score a total of ninety-six victories, twenty-one of them over four engined bombers. These markings were carried on his Fw-190 during early 1942. (James V. Crow)

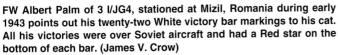

FW Albert Palm of 3 I/JG4, stationed at Mizil, Romania during early 1943 points out his twenty-two White victory bar markings to his cat. All his victories were over Soviet aircraft and had a Red star on the bottom of each bar. (James V. Crow)

Hauptman Wolfgang Lippert of Stab II JG 27 carried his twenty-one victory bars on the fin of his Bf-109E, a departure from the standard position on the rudder. He was based at Strumatal, Bulgaria during the Spring of 1941. He scored four victories in Spain and had twenty-nine when he died in December of 1941. (James V. Crow)

Oberstleutnant Heinz Baer of STAB IV/JG51 on 27 June 1942 carried a total of 113 victories on the rudder of his Bf-109F. He also flew with JG 77, JG 1, and JG 3 during his career and ended the war with 220 kills. There were small lightning flashes under the eagle with French, Russian, and British insignias. He scored sixteen of his kills with JV-44 flying the Me-262. (James V. Crow)

The Bf-109 of Oberst Hermann Graf of III/JG 52 in Russian during May of 1942 showed 108 of the 202 victories he scored during his career. The significance of the extra large bar indicated five victories scored on a single mission. Graf also flew with JG53. (James V. Crow)

This Messerschmitt Bf-109E of 3-I/JG 1 at Vecha, Germany during October of 1939. The White half moon on the fin stood for a night victory scored by Klaus Faber over a Royal Air Force Bristol Blenheim bomber. (James V. Crow)

(Right) Oberleutnant Josef Wurmheller (middle) with two new pilots who had just been awarded the Iron Cross II Class at Vannes, France during 1943, admire the score on the tail of his Fw 190A which revealed a total of seventy-five victories. The large 60 was superimposed over an RAF roundel and a small Red Star. Kill bars revealed British and five American aircraft as well (his final score was 102). He served with JG53, JG52, and JG1. Thirteen of his kills were four engined bombers. (James V. Crow)

The tail of General of Fighter Adolf Galland's Bf-109E-4 at Audembert, France during December of 1940. At that time he was flying with Stab/JG 26, although he also flew with JG 27 and JV 44. Galland went on to score a total of 103 victories. He used a light colored rectangle around his scoreboard to highlight his victory bars on the rudder of this Messerschmitt. The small circle above each bar does not appear to be the roundels of his victims. (James V. Crow)

Ofw Kurt Buhligen of II/JG 2 with his Bf-109, Yellow nine at Beaumont LeRoger, France during late 1940. Buhligen is the pilot without a hat and had a total of eight kills at this time. His scoreboard was highly unusual in that it was on a band on the rudder, rather than in the more usual vertical style of victory bar presentation. The dark band served to highlight his victory markings, all of which were scored over Royal Air Force aircraft. His Yellow side number had a thin Black outline. (James V. Crow)

Italy

While the Italian Air Force officially frowned on the use of mission and victory symbols, they still could be found on a few fighters. After the Italians became co-belligerents with the Allies, mission markings found favor on the bombers supplied by the Allies. The usual bomb symbols were used and for the most part plan view silhouettes were used on the fighters to identify kills, mostly being planted on the aircraft rudder.

This Italian Co-belligerent Air Force Martin Baltimore bomber was named *CHE NE XE POCHI CIO!!* and carried a total of eighty-one White bomb mission markers on either side of the name. The winged oil drum personal marking is a unusual for nose markings. (Ferdinado.D'Amico)

ALLO' LALI carried thrity-one White bomb mission markings on the nose just under the side windows and featured Donald Duck as the aircraft's mascot. Disney characters were favored by a number of crews during the war. The Martin Baltimore bombers were from the 28th and 132nd Gruppos of the Italian Co-belligerent Air Force which was mainly equipped with American and British aircraft. (Ferdinando D'Amico)

Serg. Magg. Tarantola of the 51st Stormo, 20th Gruppo, 151st Squadriglia points to his seven victory symbols on the rudder of his MC-202 named *Pai Banana*. Six of the silhouettes are in Yellow indicating single engine fighters while the seventh was a twin engine aircraft and was in Red. (C.M.P.R. photo via Ferdinando D'Amico)

This Messerschmitt Bf-109G-6, White 1 of the 3rd Squadriglio, 2ndGruppo Caccia was from the Aeronautica Nazionale Republicana (RSI - Northern Italian Fascist Air Force) and was flown by Maresciallo Saletti who apparently shot down a twin enginged bomber on 19 October 1944. The silhouette appears to have been an A-20 Havoc (although this is merely speculation). (Ferdinando D'Amico)

When is a kill not a kill? When it appears on the fin of a Swiss Air Force D-3801, a licensed version of the Morane-Saulnier M.S. 450 built in Switzerland! Some pilots took to painting the serial numbers of the aircraft of the fighting powers that they escorted to safe landings in Switzerland when they came into Swiss air space. These were based at Sitten Air Force Base. (Hans-Heire Stapfer)

Finland

Victory and mission markings were common in the Finnish Air Force both in the Winter War and the Continuation War. The Finns flew a number of obsolete aircraft including the Brewster Buffalo, Fokker D.21, Fiat G.50, Moraine 406, Bristol Blenheim, Ju-88, Tupelov SB-2 bis, Polikarpov I-153, and P-40 (the last three types were captured from the Russians), Hawker Hurricanes and Bf-109G. One fact that is little known is that the Finns produced five aces with more victories than MAJ R. I. Bong, the top scoring ace of the USAAF. Their top ace was Eino I. Juutilainen who racked up ninety-four victories during his career. He also managed to survive the war.

Several different types of markings were used on Finnish Air Force aircraft, some pilots used front views of their kills, others used plan view silhouettes and others included the dates of their victories. One Blenheim used a simple White bar in rows of four with the fifth bar crossing the other four, a SB-2bis had the silhouettes of the subs it sank, several pilots had a barrage balloon among their silhouettes and a SB-2bis carried three ship silhouettes on its rudder. LeLv 12, a Fokker D.21 squadron, had a White arrow planted on the rudder with 1,500 on it to indicate that LeLv 12 had flown 1,500 sorties as of 6 May 1942. Lastly, CAPT Luukkanen had what has to rank as one of the most unusual victory markings of any pilot. He cemented Karella Beer labels on the fin of his Brewster Buffalo. One can only wonder if he got to drink the beer in celebration of his victories.

LT Martti Kalima stands by the rudder of his Fokker D.21 during the Spring of 1942. His scoreboard shows victories over Russian I-153 biplanes (three), a single I-16, a single SB-2bis bomber and apparently a single Po-2. (Keski-Soumen Ilmailumuseo)

(Left) Warrent Officer Oiva E. K. Tuominen points to the spot where his twenty-third victory will be added on the rudder of his Fiat G.50 fighter. Later Tuominen was promoted to Flt. Mstr. and his final score was forty-three in the Winter War and thirty-five in the Continuation War. He flew with HLeLv 26 and 34. One of his kills was an observation balloon.

KOREA

Markings were carried on the aircraft of both sides engaged in the Korean "Police Action" and were relatively limited in variety. North Korean Peoples Air Force pilots used the Red star on their MiGs to show their victories. They were kept fairly simple and were usually carried on the nose under the cockpit in straight rows.

The United Nations forces, mainly the United States Air Force and U.S. Naval Air Force continued the Second World War practice of using the bomb symbols, camera silhouettes, and the silhouettes of enemy aircraft shot down. These did reflect the change to jets and mostly were silhouettes of MiGs. Some pilots preferred to use a Red star and these were carried in small rows on the nose under the cockpit area or around the canopy frame.

TSG Edward J. Nay of the 67th Tactical Reconnaissance Wing points to the scoreboard on the RF-80A Shooting Star that he serviced as crew chief during October of 1951. The camera silhouette mission symbols indicated that the RF-80 had flown seventy-three sorties. (USAF via David Menard)

This F-84E-20-RE Thunderjet of the 474th Fighter Bomber Group in Korea carries 180 bomb mission markers on the fuselage in Red. High total mission counts were rather common among the fighter-bomber squadrons deployed to Korea. (Larry Davis)

COL George I. Ruddell of the 39th FIS points to the large Red star added to his F-86F at K-13 after his fifth victory on 18 May 1953. It may have been the worst looking kill marking of the war and was hastily added for the benefit of the photographer as his ground crew looked on with happy smiles. (Larry Davis)

CAPT Joseph McConnell of the 16th FIS, 51st Fighter Wing flew this F-86 Sabre named *BEAUTEOUS BUTCH II*. At this time the Sabre had the silhouettes of thirteen MiG-15s. It was in this F-86 that McConnell shot down eleven of his total score. His first F-86 was named *BEAUTEOUS BUTCH* but it was lost on 12 April 1953 in the Yellow Sea when he was forced to bail out. (Larry Davis)

This Marine AD-4 of VMA-121 was based at K-6 air field in Korea during 1952. The Skyraider had racked up over 130 missions as shown on the scoreboard carried under the rear cockpit. (Larry Davis)

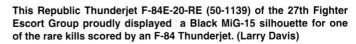

El Diablo was an F-86E of the 336th FIS, 4th Fighter Interceptor Wing and was flown by MAJ Chuck Owens at K-14 during 1953. He carried a scoreboard with eight Red Stars plus a half star, one tank and fifteen truck silhouettes. (Larry Davis)

This Republic Thunderjet F-84E-20-RE (50-1139) of the 27th Fighter Escort Group proudly displayed a Black MiG-15 silhouette for one of the rare kills scored by an F-84 Thunderjet. (Larry Davis)

This Fairchild C-119 of the 314th Troop Carrier Group had the honor of hauling the 70,000th ton of air cargo from Ashiya to Korea. Its scoreboard indicates participation in the Sunchon and Munsan-ni paradrop operations, where they dropped paratroopers and equipment. The symbols also indicate that they hauled trucks and other vehicles, oil drums, supplies and other cargo. (Via Dave Menard)

The crew of ths Superfortress of the 98th Bomb Group with 154 missions over North Korea flown as a part of the USAF Far East Bomber Command prepares to board their aircraft on 21 July 1952. The large Red Flag had the number 100 in the upper left corner with the balance of fifty-four missions indicated by the smaller Red Flags. (USAF via Larry. Davis)

Peace Time

It may come as a surprise to some people that once the bombing and shooting stopped, that did not mark the end of the use of mission symbols. Some examples are included in this section and some that we know existed but have not been able to locate photographic coverage such as missions where the Coast Guard made intercepts of drug smugglers using a Learjet, or the use of fir tree silhouettes to indicate forest fire missions on California Air Guard aircraft, simulated dog fights, and things of that nature.

HAYLIFT EXPRESS was a Curtiss C-46 Commando of the Minnesota Air Guard based at the Minneapolis Air Port. She saw emergency relief service during a serve storm that had isolated livestock in the state. Food drops in the form of hay and other forage items were carried out successfully before mechanical problems caused it to crash. Eight haylifts for cattle and ten for sheep are denoted by the two rows of mission symbols. (Via Kent Kistler)

Thirty-two Goony bird silhouettes indicate the number of the big birds that met the WV-2 Warning Star (EC-121) In the air and failed to take any sort of evasive action. These birds were a serious problem which gave the Navy on Midway Island a headache for a long time. (R.M. Hill)

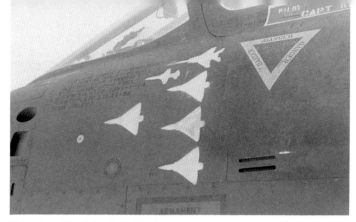

This Republic F-105D-20RE (61-0146A) of the 507th Tactical Fighter Squadron, Oklahoma Air National Guard boasts a scoreboard that tells of its successful encounters with an F-5, F-15 and four F-106s in mock combats. (John N. Campbell via Mark Bacon)

This C-124C Globemaster of the 52nd Troop Carrier Squadron featured ten penquin mission markers for flight to the Antarctic. On one of these flights it nosed over, hence the nosed down penquin. (Via Dave Menard)

(Left) NASA's Boeing 747 shuttle transporter number 905 carried these mission markings indicating Shuttle missions. The markings were carried on the 747's forward fuselage just above the Blue stripe above the first and second windows just to the rear of the forward cabin door. Shuttle missions were colored Red and Black which showed the Shuttle attached to the 747 and in Dark Blue for aerial drops and in Light Blue for drops without the Shuttle's protective tail cone in place. (via David Menard and Boeing)

This surprised bird was carried by a T-34B flown by Lou Drendel of the Lima Lima aerobatic team to indicate a bird strike. The Mentor was credited with one confirmed Seagull kill. (Bob Krenkel)

VIET NAM

Both Air Force and Navy fighters used various types of enemy aircraft silhouettes, some were superimposed over a larger Red star, some carried the date and type of enemy aircraft painted either on the plane silhouette or in the Red star. In some cases the Navy used an aircraft silhouette but carried the total number of enemy aircraft destroyed by the entire squadron rather than an individual pilot.

Lightning flashes were used to denote ECM or electronic warfare sorties, the usual bomb symbol was still high in popularity in both services for regular bomb runs. The USAF also used Red stars outlined in either White or Red to show up more clearly on camouflaged aircraft. The Forward Air Controllers were apt to use silhouettes of the enemy vehicles they helped destroy. Other symbols were in use at various times and places, with even a few individual types appearing from time to time.

The North Vietnamese Air Force, for the most part, seemed to use a standard Red star for kill markings

This Douglas A-4C Skyhawk of VA-56 was flown by LT Dale Palmer. The Skyhawk had a scoreboard with a total of 114 bomb mission symbols. (Duane A. Kasulka)

An F-8H Crusader (BuNo 148648) flown by LCDR Bob Kirkwood of VF-24 aboard USS HANCOCK (CVA-19) featured four silhouettes of MiG-17s on the ventral fin. VF-24 shot down four MiGs on 21 July 1967 and Kirkwood was credited with one of them. (Duane A. Kasulka)

Six Mig kills are recorded on the splitter plate of the this F-4D Phantom plus what appears to be a Ryan Firebee kill. This F-4D flew with the 555th Tactical Fighter Squadron and was later assigned to the 8th TFW at Osan AB, Korea (David W. Menard)

This A-7A Corsair II of VA-147 Argonauts was one of the first fleet operational Corsair IIs and began combat operations in December of 1967 aboard the USS RANGER. This A-7 flew eleven bomber escort missions as shown by the bombs superimposed over the silhouette of an aircraft. (Duane A. Kasulka)

LCOL Fred A. Baeffner and 1LT Michael R. Bever shot down a MiG-17 with an AIM-7 missile on 13 May 1967. At the time, Haeffner was on temporary duty with the 453rd TFS, 8th Tactical Fighter Wing, although he was assigned to the 390th TFS of the 366th TFW. The kill was credited to the F-4C of the 8th TFW and had the kill painted on the splitter plate. The aircraft was also credited with a second kill at a later date. (CAPT Bernie Moore II)

Operation DESERT STORM

Durring Operation DESERT STORM, the custom of carrying mission and kill markings was revived. Some new symbols began appearing to mark the new technology of this war. Missile markings became more common, as did symbols for radar sites. A-10s carried large scoreboards with everything from Armored Personal Carriers to helicopters. Helicopters carried mission markings, such as mines or enemy prisoners carried back to POW camps. Kills markings were usually limited to Iraqi flag markings displayed on the fuselage under the cockpit.

British aircraft carried some of the most elaborate scoreboards with different symbols to indicate the type of mission or even the type of bombs carried.

LT Richard Dann and LT Gil Storey flew this SH-60B in the Persian Gulf during Operation DESERT STORM. On one patrol AW1 McEaulley spotted a drifting mine, which was destroyed by EOD personnel. A week later LT Dann spotted a second mine, which was also destroyed. The crew painted their helo with two Black mine symbols to record their kills. (Via Richard Dann)

(Left) A-10 Thunderbolt IIs carried elaborate nose art and scoreboards to record their accomplishments during Operation DESERT STORM. This A-10A named DESERT ROSE had a scoreboard that reflected fifteen tanks, ten armored vehicles, nineteen guns, one self-propelled gun, eight radar sites and seventeen trucks. (Dana Bell)

This Marine crops A-6E Intruder destroyed one bridge, four small trucks, two large trucks, two field guns, one self-propelled gun and one towed gun during Operation DESERT STORM. (N.J. Waters III)

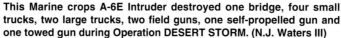